The Untouched Feeling

Two strangers. One train. A journey of unspoken feelings

Younus Ali

To my wife Sunheela,

This book, these words, and every story within these pages wouldn't have come to life without your presence and encouragement.

This book is as much yours as it is mine, and I'm honored to walk this path with you. Thank you for believing in me, for sharing your life with me, and for being the journey.

Foreword

"The Untouched Feeling" is a journey of the body, mind and soul.

The sweet irony is that, while writing about his and his partner's Untouched Feelings, the author delicately Touches uncountable Feelings of different readers.

PHYSICAL JOURNEY WHERE THE DESTINATION HOLDS THE CONNECTION OF SOULS.

Proofreading is a task, which actually became an enthusiasm as the intricate and graceful definitions & descriptions of 'feelings' kept me spell-bound, quite a number of times. Ignored moments, slipped chances, that could be altered, should be noticed, taken care of, to make life as beautiful as ever possible.

Life is often a journey of unspoken emotions, hidden struggles, and quiet realizations. Many of us walk through our days carrying burdens only we know, feeling moments of connection that are fleeting, fragile, yet profoundly impactful. We meet people who touch our lives in ways we didn't see coming, leaving an indelible mark on our journey, even if only for a moment.

— Dr. Sunheela K. Ali

Preface

"The Untouched Feeling" is a story about two such people—two strangers with lives weighed down by pain, disappointment, and fear. Aryan and Meera meet in an ordinary place, under ordinary circumstances, but what unfolds between them is anything but ordinary.

What makes this story unique is its roots in true events. As the author, I am both a narrator and the endurer, sharing a journey inspired by my own life experiences. The reflections within these pages are not merely words; they are pieces of real lives, real struggles, and real feelings, hidden beneath the surface of daily existence.

This book is for anyone who has ever felt lost, who has ever faced the choice between staying in the comfort of familiarity and stepping into the unknown. It's about the courage to confront the untouched parts of ourselves—the fears, the doubts, the memories we've tucked away—and what it means to share those hidden pieces with another soul.

So, as you turn these pages, consider this: perhaps the connections that change us the most are the ones we least expect. And perhaps, hidden within the ordinary, are the moments that will help us find our extraordinary selves.

I hope this novel resonates with you, the reader, as deeply as the experiences it is based on resonate with me.

Thank you for embarking on this journey with me.

Prologue

There are moments in life that catch us off guard, moments where everything changes without warning. Plans unravel, expectations shatter, and the world as we know it tilts on its axis, leaving us scrambling to understand what went wrong.

This story begins at one of those moments.

Two strangers, Aryan and Meera, boarded a train that should have taken them to nowhere special, just another stop in their long exhausting lives. Both running from – memories, from regrets, from versions of themselves they could no longer bear.

As their journey continued, Aryan and Meera were forced to make a choice; remain in the safety of their pain or take a leap of faith into the unknown – a place where vulnerability could either break them or set them free.

This is the story of what happens when we stop running. When we pause long enough to look someone in the eye and realize that they, too, are fighting their own battles.

And in that moment, when everything is on the line, we're faced with a question; Do we risk it all? Or do we let the moment pass by, never knowing what could have been?

Contents

The Station	10
The Real Relationship	43
Attraction – The Lack of it	52
The Oppressor is the Oppressed	76
Mirror- What it says	95
Who is on the other side	110
The Expectations	127
The Deliberation on Love	144
The Stolen Time	167
The Availability	175
The Paradigm of Problem	186
Trust - The Emotional Collapse	193
The War Within	198
A Moment	205
The Fear of Losing	212
The Leap of Faith	219

The train slowed, a heavy hiss echoing through the silence of the station. Aryan stood at the door, his heart pounding in sync with the slowing rhythm of the wheels. His hand hovered over the metal rail, fingers gripping tightly, as if letting go would mean losing something he couldn't name.

This was it. His stop.

The rain had stopped moments ago, leaving the platform wet and glistening in the muted light of dawn. The air was thick with the smell of damp concrete and earth, mingling with the distant sound of voices, muffled and far away. Aryan felt engulfed of everything behind him—the life he was leaving, the one he wasn't sure he wanted to return to.

He took a step forward, then hesitated. Was she still here?

A thousand thoughts raced through his mind. Meera. He had left her sitting in the carriage, lost in her thoughts, just as lost as he was in his own. They hadn't spoken in hours. Not since that brief exchange—where everything felt like it was on the edge of falling apart. His heart clenched at the memory, the unspoken words hanging between them like ghosts.

He exhaled, a slow, deliberate breath. The doors hissed open, and the cold air hit his face like a slap. The platform stretched out before him, empty but fully enveloped in his indecision. He stepped off the train, his shoes splashing lightly in the shallow puddles left behind by the rain.

It felt surreal. Like he was caught between worlds. The one he had known—filled with betrayal, loss, and the endless ache of missed chances—and this new, uncertain path. Was Meera part of it? Or was he meant to walk away now, leaving it all behind?

He glanced around, scanning the station.

Where was she?

The Station

The rain was relentless. Heavy drops slammed against the window, each one echoing the quiet frustration in Aryan's mind. He had spent the last hour staring blankly at the empty document on his laptop, the cursor blinking as if mocking him.

How many times had he sat like this, willing the words to come, yet finding nothing? Seven years had passed since he'd first thought about writing a book, but every time he tried, something inside him froze. The thoughts, once vivid in his mind, would blur into incoherence the moment he placed his fingers on the keyboard. Tonight was no different.

He closed the laptop, the silence in the room growing louder as the rain intensified. "Not tonight," he whispered to himself. But even as he said it, something stirred deep within him. He couldn't let this be another failed attempt. He wouldn't let his doubts win again.

Suddenly, almost impulsively, Aryan stood up. He reached for his wallet on the counter, his hand trembling slightly. The rain outside mirrored the storm in his mind—a torrent of unresolved feelings, frustrations, and an overwhelming sense of being stuck. He didn't know what made him grab his things and head out the door. All he knew was that if he didn't leave now, he might never write again. His heart raced as he shut the door behind him, slamming it hard enough to make his cat, Simba, leap off the windowsill in fright.

"Sorry, Simba," Aryan muttered, already halfway down the stairs. Simba, a scruffy orange tabby, was used to Aryan's erratic behavior, but Aryan couldn't help but feel a pang of guilt. He could still see the startled look on the cat's face, wide-eyed and wary. It reminded him of himself—always on edge, always expecting something to go wrong.

He sprinted down the staircase, his footsteps echoing in the stairwell. The cold wind hit him hard as he emerged from the building, cutting through the thin fabric of his shirt. He hadn't even thought to grab a jacket, but he didn't care. The train wouldn't wait, and neither could he. As he reached the street, his auto driver was already waiting for him, looking as impatient as ever.

The rain beat against the roof like an unforgiving drum, each drop heavy and unrelenting. Aryan shoved his phone into his pocket, glancing anxiously at the time. He hadn't left himself much of a cushion; the train was scheduled to depart in twenty minutes, and the station wasn't exactly close. The auto rickshaw driver, an older man with a perpetually sour expression, looked as if he'd rather be anywhere but here. His knuckles were white as they gripped the steering wheel, and Aryan wondered, not for the first time, what kind of day this man had endured. "Railway station, and fast," Aryan urged, his voice catching in the urgency of the moment.

Without a word, the driver floored the accelerator, and Aryan was immediately flung back against the seat as the vehicle shot forward. The narrow streets were slick with rain, their reflections blurring the city lights into streaks of gold and red. The driver maneuvered through the traffic with the precision of a man who had done this a thousand times before, but to Aryan, it felt like madness.

He gripped the sides of the seat as the auto swerved past honking cars and sputtering motorcycles, narrowly avoiding a collision with a truck that loomed out of nowhere. The engine roared louder, the sound drowning out the cacophony of the city around them. The rain was so heavy it was like driving through a curtain of water, the windshield wipers working furiously but barely making a difference.

Aryan glanced out the side, watching as street vendors scrambled to pack up their carts, plastic sheets flapping wildly in the wind. The rain-soaked streets were chaos—puddles the size of small lakes formed on the sides of the road, and people struggled with broken umbrellas, trying to shield themselves from the storm.

The traffic, however, was relentless. Cars honked their horns, motorcycles squeezed through impossibly small gaps, and everyone seemed in a hurry to escape the rain. Aryan's stomach felt in knots with each reckless turn the driver made. At this rate, he felt like the rain might swallow them whole before they even made it to the station.

"Are we going to make it?" Aryan asked, trying to mask the panic rising in his chest.

The driver didn't answer, simply nodding and making a sharp left, darting down a narrower lane that seemed almost too small for the auto. It was a gamble, and Aryan's heart leapt into his throat as the auto squeezed past a delivery truck, barely clearing the edge. The engine groaned in protest as they hit another puddle, spraying water across the window. For a moment, Aryan thought they might stall, but the driver pushed on, weaving through back streets and cutting across lanes like a man possessed. They passed red lights, careened over potholes, and even narrowly avoided a dog that darted out into the street. It was a race against time, and Aryan felt like he was holding on to his dear life, white-knuckled and wide-eyed.

Finally, the station came into view, looming in the distance like a beacon of hope. The rain showed no sign of stopping, but Aryan's pulse quickened as the driver screeched into the station's entrance with a final, reckless burst of speed.

The station was packed with people, all moving in different directions, their umbrellas clashing like weapons as they fought against the downpour. Aryan shoved a few crumpled bills into the driver's hand without waiting for change. He barely heard the driver mutter something about the weather, already leaping out of the auto and running for the entrance.

The rain was merciless. He felt each drop crushing down on him as he ran, his shoes slipping against the slick pavement, sending cold splashes of water up his legs. The station loomed ahead; its old clock tower partially obscured by the thick curtain of rain. His heart pounded, his breath quickening as he dodged past people, his mind entirely focused on catching the train.

When he reached the ticket counters, the large overhead board glowed red with numbers and letters. He squinted through the rain. His train was there, scheduled to depart in a few minutes.

Inside the station, chaos reigned. People rushed in all directions, drenched and frustrated, the air thick with the smell of wet clothes and impatience. Vendors shouted, luggage wheels clattered across the floor, and announcements echoed over the loudspeakers, half-lost in the storm's roar.

Aryan barely registered it all as he darted past the crowds, heading straight for Platform 4. The sound of the train engine's slow rumble reached him, and his pulse quickened. Was it already leaving?

His shoes squeaked loudly against the slick marble floors as he sprinted toward the platform. The train was still there, the engine humming softly, preparing for departure. He skidded to a halt beside his coach, gasping for air. The metal door loomed before him, the metal handle felt cold, and the door opened with a hiss.
With a final push, Aryan hoisted himself inside, his heart hammering against his ribs. He made it.

The interior of the coach was dimly lit and relatively calm compared to the frenzy outside. A wave of relief washed over him, but he was drenched to the bone, his clothes clinging to his skin. He took a few deep breaths, trying to calm himself as he made his way down the narrow aisle, searching for his berth.

The coach was quiet, save for the occasional murmur of passengers settling into their seats. He noticed a few familiar scenes—a weary-looking elderly couple stowing their luggage, a young couple speaking in hushed tones, laughing softly at some private joke. But then, at the far end of the coach, he saw her.

She sat by the window, her seat bathed in the soft glow of the dim light overhead. Her profile was delicate yet striking. The rain-soaked glass cast reflections across her face, creating a soft halo of light around her. Her hair, long and dark, fell in soft waves over her shoulders, some strands brushing gently against her cheek as she gazed out into the storm.

There was something ethereal about her, something that made Aryan pause in his steps. He watched as she raised a hand to tuck a loose strand of hair behind her ear, the movement graceful, almost absent-minded, as though she was lost in thoughts too deep to surface from. Her fingers were long, elegant, and the way she touched her hair was as if she was accustomed to handling fragile things.

Her beauty was understated, quiet, the kind that didn't announce itself loudly but grew on you the more you looked. Her features were sharp yet soft—her lips full, her nose small, and her eyes... Her eyes, when she finally turned to glance at the platform outside, were like dark pools, deep and unreadable.

Meera. The name fit her, though Aryan didn't know it yet. But there was an air of quiet mystery about her, something that stirred the lingering embers of curiosity within him. She seemed so peaceful, so composed, in contrast to the storm raging outside. The dim light from the overhead lamp cast soft shadows across her face, accentuating her high cheekbones and the gentle curve of her jaw.

Her gaze never left the window, even as the train began to lurch forward, the platform slowly sliding away from view. Aryan felt a sudden urge to sit near her, to speak to her, but his body betrayed him, keeping him rooted where he stood. For a moment, the rest of the train seemed to fade away, the noise of the wheels on the tracks distant and muffled. All he could focus on was her, this woman who sat with such quiet elegance, watching the world outside pass her by, as if she were a part of something far larger than the here and now.

The train jerked forward, a loud screech filling the air as it finally departed the station. Aryan's feet moved without him realizing it, guiding him to his seat, but even as he settled in, his mind remained on the woman at the end of the coach.

Who was she? Why did she seem so distant, so

unreachable? He didn't know. But something told him that this encounter, this moment on the train, held some beginning.

As the train pulled away from the station, Aryan leaned back in his seat, feeling the vibration of the engine rumble beneath him. The lights inside the coach flickered for a moment before settling into a soft, yellow glow, casting long shadows across the narrow aisle. Outside, the rain drummed steadily against the window, merging with the rhythmic clatter of the wheels on the tracks. The storm raged on, but inside the train, everything seemed still—calm, even.

His eyes kept drifting back to her. There was something about her presence that tugged at him, a quiet elegance that stood out even in the dim, confined space of the train. He didn't understand it, but he felt it. Aryan had always been a careful observer of people—something that came naturally to him after years of working in IT, where attention to detail was second nature. But this woman... she was different. An invisible tension clung to her stillness, as if she carried the world on her shoulders but wore it with grace.

She hadn't moved much since they departed. Her gaze remained fixed on the window, where the raindrops raced each other down the glass. Every now and then, she would lift her hand to brush away a stray lock of hair that had fallen over her face, but other than that, she was motionless, lost in her thoughts. From where he sat, Aryan could see the subtle breathing, the gentle curve of her jaw, and the way her lips pressed together in a soft line—neither a smile nor a frown.

The coach around them was quieting down. Passengers were beginning to settle in for the night, adjusting their seats and pulling out thin blankets. The elderly couple across the aisle whispered softly to one another, their voices barely audible over the noise of the train. The younger couple, who had been chatting animatedly earlier, had now leaned into each other, their heads resting together in a tender moment of shared exhaustion.

Aryan shifted in his seat, feeling the cool air of the coach wrap around him. He was still damp from the rain, his shirt sticking uncomfortably to his back, but the cold didn't bother him. Not really. His mind was elsewhere, spinning with thoughts of the journey ahead and the woman seated just a few rows away.

Who was she? Aryan couldn't shake the question from his mind. She wasn't just another passenger, that much was clear. There was something deeper beneath her calm exterior, something that intrigued him. He tried to imagine what kind of life she led. Was she traveling for work? To visit family? Or was she, like him, running away from something—or toward something?

He turned his gaze back to the window, watching the blurred landscape fly past in the darkness. The rain outside seemed relentless, each drop hitting the glass with the force of his own unsettled thoughts. Aryan had always found solace in the rain, its steady rhythm helping to drown out the noise in his mind. But tonight, it only amplified his restlessness.

There was a part of him that wanted to get up, walk over to her, and introduce himself. He had always been curious about people, always willing to strike up a conversation, even with strangers. Yet something held him back this time. Maybe it was the way she seemed so completely absorbed in her own world, her own thoughts. He didn't want to intrude on that. Not yet.

The train jolted slightly, pulling Aryan from his reverie. He glanced at his phone, checking the time. It was late—later than he thought—and they had a long journey ahead of them. He leaned back in his seat, trying to relax, but his mind refused to settle.

As he stared out into the dark, rain-soaked night, he couldn't help but think about his own journey. This trip wasn't just about reaching somewhere. It wasn't even about attending some family event that awaited him. No, this was about something more—something personal. Something he hadn't fully acknowledged yet.

He thought of his parents, of the betrayal that still stung even after all these years. The way they had taken everything from him—his earnings, his trust, his sense of security. Aryan had worked his whole life, saved every penny, planning for a future that was ripped away from him in an instant. When they squandered his money, leaving him with nothing, it wasn't just his finances that were destroyed. It was his entire foundation—his faith in family, in people, in life.

The worst part wasn't even the loss. It was the silence that followed. No one had come to help him. No one had stood by his side when he needed them most. Not sisters, not brothers, not even distant relatives. He had been utterly alone, left to pick up the pieces of his shattered life on his own.

He closed his eyes, feeling the familiar heaviness of anger and sadness pressing against his chest. Why was he thinking about this now? Was it the rain, or the quiet hum of the train, or maybe even the presence of the woman across the aisle that stirred these old emotions to the surface? He didn't know. But it hurt, even now, after all this time.

The train jolted again, and Aryan opened his eyes, glancing toward the woman once more. Meera. He didn't know her name yet, but in his mind, she was already Meera. There was something about her presence that calmed him, even as his thoughts raced uncontrollably.

She shifted slightly in her seat, her hand moving to adjust her shawl, which had slipped off her shoulder. Aryan noticed the small details—the way the fabric draped over her, the delicate way she held herself, as if every movement was purposeful, graceful. Her fingers were slender, elegant, her nails painted a soft shade of pink that stood out against the dark tones of the shawl.

For a brief moment, her eyes flicked toward him, and Aryan felt his breath catch. Her eyes were dark and deep, like the rain-soaked night outside, filled with stories and emotions he couldn't even begin to understand. She didn't smile, but there was a kindness in her gaze, a softness that made him feel as though she had seen him—truly seen him—for just that moment.

And then she turned away, her attention drawn back to the window, back to the world outside.

The silence between them lingered, thick with the unspoken tension of two people who had yet to meet, yet already felt connected in some strange, inexplicable way. Aryan didn't know what would happen next. He didn't know if he would find the courage to speak to her, to ask her name, to share even a small part of the story that had been building inside him for years.

But what he did know was that this journey—this unexpected encounter—felt like the beginning of something. Whether it was fate or coincidence, he couldn't say. But something in him stirred, a quiet voice that whispered that this moment, this chance meeting, might change everything.

The train moved steadily through the night, its rhythmic chugging a constant backdrop to the swirling thoughts in Aryan's mind. The world outside was a blur, dark and shapeless, with only the rain tapping persistently against the windows, as if it, too, wanted to be heard. Inside the coach, the low hum of the engine mixed with the occasional rustle of passengers shifting in their seats or pulling their blankets tighter against the chill air.

But Aryan was far from settled.

He couldn't stop thinking about the woman across the aisle. Meera, as he had already begun to think of her. Every few minutes, his eyes darted back to her, catching fleeting glimpses of her as she sat perfectly still, as if the storm outside had no power over her. He wondered what she was thinking—what was holding her attention so deeply that she hadn't even glanced away from the window.

There was a quiet grace to her that fascinated him, but more than that, there was a heaviness, too. An unspoken gravity that Aryan recognized all too well. It was the same burden he carried, the same gnawing sense of loss and longing that had haunted him for years.

He shifted in his seat, uncomfortable not just because of the damp clothes still clinging to his skin but because of the memories that were beginning to surface. Memories he had spent a lifetime trying to bury.

His mind wandered back to those dark days when his world had crumbled. He remembered how it had felt to watch everything he had worked for disappear in an instant. The betrayal by his parents had been the final blow, the one that had shattered his faith in people, in life. After they had squandered his savings, he had been left with nothing—no safety net, no support, and worst of all, no one to turn to.

He had been alone. Utterly, painfully alone.

He swallowed hard, trying to push the thoughts away, but they clung to him like the dampness of his clothes. There were moments when the anger would rise again, unbidden, and fill him with a bitterness so deep it left him hollow. And then there were moments like this—quiet, reflective moments—when the sadness would creep in, soft and insidious, wrapping around him like a cold fog.

He closed his eyes for a moment, trying to breathe through it, but the quiet around him only made the memories louder. He had come on this journey to escape those thoughts, to find some kind of peace, but instead, he felt more restless than ever.

When he opened his eyes again, the first thing he saw was Meera.

Her posture had changed slightly—she was now leaning forward, her elbows resting on her knees, her fingers laced together in front of her. There was something so delicate about her, but at the same time, something strong. Her hair had fallen forward, a few strands brushing against her face, but she made no move to push them away.

Instead, she simply gazed out the window, watching the rain with a faraway look in her eyes. The dim light cast shadows across her face, highlighting the sharp angles of her cheekbones and the soft curve of her lips. Aryan couldn't help but be drawn to her. There was a quiet beauty to her, an elegance that seemed both natural and unattainable, as if she belonged to a world just out of reach.

He wanted to speak to her. The urge was growing stronger with each passing moment, but something held him back. It wasn't just his own nervousness or the fear of rejection—it was something deeper, something unspoken. It was the sense that she, too, was carrying a burden, and he didn't want to intrude on that.

But still, the question lingered in his mind: Who was she?

He wondered if her journey was anything like his. Was she running from something, or trying to find something? What stories did those dark eyes hold? What pain was she hiding behind that calm, composed exterior? He didn't know, but he wanted to.

A soft sound broke through the quiet of the coach. Aryan turned slightly and saw that the elderly couple across the aisle were whispering to each other again, their voices barely audible over the hum of the train. The old man's hand rested on his wife's, their fingers intertwined, a gesture so simple yet so full of tenderness that it made Aryan felt a sharp pang of sorrow gripping him.

He hadn't had anything like that in years. Not since his world had fallen apart. Not since the betrayal.

He looked away, unable to bear the sight of such quiet intimacy. The loneliness settled in again, heavier now, pressing down on him with a force that was almost suffocating. He had spent so much of his life building walls, keeping people out, and now, sitting in this dimly lit train with strangers all around him, he realized just how isolated he had become.

And yet, here was Meera. Another stranger, yes, but something about her felt familiar. As if they shared some kind of unspoken connection, some kind of shared pain.

Before he could stop himself, Aryan glanced at her again. This time, their eyes met.

It was brief—just a flicker of a moment—but in that moment, something passed between them. A recognition, perhaps. Or maybe just a shared understanding. Aryan couldn't be sure, but he felt it. The pull between them.

Meera's gaze lingered for a moment before she looked away, her attention drawn back to the rain outside. But that one look had been enough. Aryan felt his heart quicken, his pulse racing with the sudden realization that he couldn't stay silent much longer. He needed to speak to her. He needed to know who she was.

But how could he approach her? What could he possibly say to a woman like that?

As the train rumbled on, Aryan's mind raced, searching for the right words, the right moment. But for now, all he could do was wait. Wait for the right moment to come.

The train's rhythmic sway seemed to slow the world around him, but inside Aryan, the turbulence only grew. He stared out the window, though he could see nothing but his own reflection in the rain-soaked glass. The dim light in the coach made his reflection ghostly—his face barely recognizable, like a shadow of the man he once was.

How had he ended up here? To become this endless routine of numbing himself to the world? He had once believed in things—in people, in trust, in the future. He had once imagined that.

It wasn't just about this train journey. No, it was more than that. How had his life's hard work and loyalty would be rewarded, that family meant something, that love could last. But somewhere along the way, all of that had been shattered.

He had trusted his parents—loved them—and they had destroyed him without a second thought. The betrayal had been so deep, so incomprehensible, that Aryan still didn't know how to process it. It wasn't just the money they had taken—it was the sense of safety, the belief that someone in the world had his back. That had all crumbled with one decision, one selfish act, and Aryan had been left alone to pick up the pieces.

And he had never truly recovered.

He glanced at Meera again. Her presence felt like a quiet echo of his own loneliness. She looked like someone who had also lost something, someone who carried her own luggage of unspoken pain. But how could he know that for sure? Was he just projecting his own emptiness onto her? Or was there really something between them, some kind of shared understanding that neither had acknowledged yet?

He watched as her fingers lightly traced the edge of the window. It was such a simple movement, but it seemed to hold meaning, as though she, too, was lost in her own thoughts, her own memories. Aryan felt a surge of empathy for her, though he still didn't know anything about her.

The train hit a slight bump on the tracks, and Aryan's hand brushed against the armrest, grounding him for a moment. He took a deep breath, trying to steady himself, but the ache in his chest remained. He had spent so much time trying to move past the pain, trying to focus on his career, on rebuilding what had been taken from him, but no matter how far he ran, the past was always there, lingering in the background like an unwanted shadow.

The rain outside showed no signs of stopping. It pounded against the windows with relentless force, as though the world outside was trying to wash everything away. Aryan found some strange comfort in the storm. The rain mirrored the chaos inside him, and yet it also brought a sense of cleansing, of release.

"Are you okay?"

The voice startled him.

It was soft, hesitant, but it broke through the steady hum of the train like a jolt. Aryan turned his head, his heart skipping a beat as he realized it was her.

Meera was looking directly at him.

For a moment, Aryan couldn't find his voice. Her eyes were even more striking up close—dark and deep, but soft around the edges, like she was genuinely concerned. He blinked, feeling a flush of embarrassment rise to his cheeks. How long had he been staring out the window? Had she noticed him watching her?

"I—uh, yes. I'm fine," Aryan stammered, sitting up a little straighter, though he was far from feeling fine.

She gave him a small smile, one that didn't quite reach her eyes. "You looked… lost. I thought I'd ask."

Aryan swallowed hard. Lost. Yes, that was exactly how he felt, and hearing it spoken aloud made the word sit heavy in the air between them. He didn't know how to respond to that, how to tell her that he had felt lost for years.

"I suppose I am," he admitted after a pause, his voice low. "A little lost."

Meera's gaze lingered on him for a moment longer, as if she was weighing his words, trying to understand what he meant. Her expression softened, and she gave a small nod, as though she knew exactly what he was feeling.

"Me too," she said quietly.

There it was. The connection. The unspoken understanding that Aryan had sensed from the beginning. It was real. She was lost, just like him. Maybe for different reasons, but the emotion was the same, and it hung between them, raw and unguarded.

For a few moments, neither of them said anything more. The silence wasn't uncomfortable, though. In fact, Aryan felt strangely at ease, as if her simple admission had opened a door between them, a door neither had been brave enough to open until now.

He wasn't sure what to say next. He wasn't good at this—talking about his emotions, about the things that had broken him. It was easier to keep it all buried, to pretend like it didn't hurt as much as it did. But sitting here, with the rain pouring down outside and Meera looking at him with eyes that seemed to see more than he wanted to reveal, Aryan felt something shift inside him.

"I'm Aryan," he said finally, his voice quiet but steady.

Meera's lips curved into a soft smile. "Meera."

Aryan nodded, his heart still racing a little from the unexpected conversation. Meera. The name suited her. It was soft, understated, but there was strength in it, too. He didn't know why, but hearing her name made him feel as though he had already known her for longer than just these few moments.

"I suppose we're both on this train for a reason," Meera said, her gaze drifting back to the window. "Maybe we'll figure out what that reason is."

Aryan didn't respond right away. He was still processing the fact that she had spoken to him at all, let alone that she had opened up to him. But as the rain continued to fall, and the train rumbled steadily along the tracks, he found himself hoping that maybe—just maybe—this journey was about more than just getting from one place to another.

Maybe this was the beginning of something neither of them had expected.

For a long while, they sat in silence again, both of them staring out at the rain as it streaked down the glass, casting ghostly shadows across the coach. Aryan felt the gravitation of Meera's presence beside him, but it wasn't heavy or uncomfortable. It was grounding, in a way that surprised him. He had spent so long pushing people away, isolating himself behind walls he had built to protect whatever was left of his heart, that he had almost forgotten what it felt like to be seen by someone.

It was a strange feeling. Almost disorienting.

He turned slightly, his gaze settling on her profile. Meera looked so calm, so composed, but there was a sadness beneath that stillness, a quiet sorrow that seemed to linger just beneath the surface. He didn't know what it was—what had caused that sadness—but he knew it was there. He could feel it, as if it echoed his own.

"You said you're lost, too," Aryan said softly, breaking the silence. "Do you mind if I ask why?"

Meera didn't respond immediately. Her fingers traced the edge of the window, her eyes distant, as if she were somewhere far away. Aryan wondered if he had crossed a line, if he had asked too much too soon. But before he could apologize, she spoke.

"It's a long story," she said, her voice quiet but steady. "And it's… complicated."

Aryan nodded, understanding. Weren't they all complicated? Everyone carried their own stories, their own burdens, and those stories were rarely simple. But there was something about the way Meera spoke—so calmly, so matter-of-factly—that made Aryan feel like she had carried her burden for a long time. Maybe too long.

"We have time," Aryan said, a small smile tugging at the corners of his lips. "It's a long journey."

Meera turned to look at him then, her eyes soft but serious. She studied him for a moment, as if deciding whether or not to trust him with her story. Aryan held her gaze, trying to show her that he understood, that he wasn't just asking to pass the time. He genuinely wanted to know.

Finally, Meera sighed, leaning back in her seat. "I guess you could say I'm running away," she admitted, her voice barely above a whisper. "Or maybe I'm just trying to find something… I don't know anymore."

Aryan's heart felt heavy. He had felt that way for so long running from something, but never quite sure what he was running toward. It was a feeling that had haunted him ever since his life had fallen apart.

"I think I understand that" Aryan said softly, his gaze drifting back to the window. "It's hard to know where you're going when you're not sure where you've been."

Meera nodded; her expression thoughtful. For a moment, they were both silent again, the rain filling the space between them. Aryan wondered what had happened to her—what had made her feel so lost, so disconnected from the world. But he didn't push. He knew better than anyone that some stories took time to tell, and that not all of them could be told in one sitting.

"I've been in an abusive marriage for years," Meera said quietly, almost as if she were speaking to herself rather than to him. Aryan's heart skipped a beat, the burden of her words hitting him like a punch to the chest. He hadn't expected that—hadn't expected her to be so open, so vulnerable, so soon.

"I'm sorry," Aryan said, his voice thick with emotion. He didn't know what else to say. There were no words that could make up for the kind of pain she must have endured, for the years she had spent trapped in a situation that had drained her of so much.

Meera's gaze softened, but she didn't smile. "Thank you," she said, her voice steady. "But I'm not looking for pity. I'm looking for… a way out. I've been studying for my PhD, trying to find something—some kind of meaning, some kind of future—but it's been hard. I don't know if I'm doing the right thing, or if

I'm just running away from something I should be facing."

Aryan nodded slowly, feeling her words resonate deep within him. He had been running, too, hadn't he? Running from the pain of betrayal, from the loneliness that had consumed him after everything had fallen apart. And like Meera, he wasn't sure if he was running toward something or simply trying to escape the ghosts of his past.

"You're stronger than you think," Aryan said quietly, surprising himself with the certainty in his voice. "You wouldn't be here if you weren't."

Meera looked at him then, her eyes softening just a little. She gave a small, sad smile. "Maybe," she said, her voice barely audible over the sound of the rain. "Maybe."

They sat in silence after that, both of them lost in their own thoughts, the air of their shared confession settling between them like an unspoken understanding. The train continued its steady journey through the night, the sound of the wheels on the tracks lulling the other passengers to sleep. But Aryan and Meera remained awake, both of them aware that something had shifted in the air between them.

For the first time in a long time, Aryan felt a glimmer of hope. He didn't know what it meant, or where this journey would take him, but he knew that something had changed. Meera had opened a door he hadn't even realized was there, and now, he wasn't sure he could close it again.

Maybe that was okay.

As the train sped into the night, Aryan felt the strain of the past start to lift, just a little. He wasn't sure what the future held, but for the first time in years, he felt like he wasn't alone.

And for now, that was enough.

The night felt endless. The rain still fell steadily against the windows of the train, though it had softened to a gentle patter, as if the storm had finally begun to tire. Inside the coach, the dim lights wavered as if struggling to stay on, casting a faint glow over the sleeping passengers. Aryan couldn't sleep. His mind was racing, tumbling over itself with thoughts he hadn't let surface in years. Meera's words echoed in his head, stirring emotions he had long buried.

Abusive marriage. Betrayal. Running away.

He had never expected to meet someone like her on this journey. Someone who could look him in the eyes and understand, without needing to explain everything. She had opened up to him in a way that had felt both natural and terrifying, and now he found himself wondering how it was possible to feel so connected to someone he had only just met.

But it wasn't just about her. It was about him, too.

Meera's story had brought Aryan face-to-face with his own demons—the betrayal of his parents, the years of isolation, the constant sense that he had lost something he could never get back. He had spent so long avoiding those feelings, pretending that he was fine, that he had moved on. But in the quiet of this night, with the train rumbling steadily beneath him and the rain tapping lightly against the window, he couldn't escape them anymore.

His parents' betrayal had broken something inside him.

He could still remember the day it happened—the moment everything fell apart. He had trusted them, believed in them. After all, they were his parents. The people who had raised him, supported him, who had always been there for him. But that trust had been shattered when he found out that they had gambled away everything he had worked for—his life's savings, his future. They had left him with nothing, and worst of all, they had offered no apology, no explanation.

It had been years since then, but the wound still felt fresh, like it had never truly healed. How could it? How could he ever trust anyone again after something like that? How could he ever believe that people were capable of genuine love, of loyalty, when the very people who were supposed to love him most had betrayed him so completely?

Aryan sighed, running a hand through his hair, felt the load of betrayal on his shoulder, even now. He had tried to move on, tried to rebuild his life, but there had always been a wall between him and the rest of the world—a wall he had built to protect himself from ever being hurt like that again.

But now, sitting here with Meera, Aryan couldn't help but wonder if he had been wrong. Maybe the wall hadn't protected him at all. Maybe it had only kept him trapped, alone.

"I don't know what to believe anymore," Aryan murmured, his voice barely audible above the sound of the rain. He wasn't even sure if he was speaking to Meera or just to himself.

Meera turned her head slightly, her eyes soft but curious. "What do you mean?"

Aryan hesitated. How could he explain it? How could he put into words the deep, gnawing sense of loss that had haunted him for so long? But something about Meera made him want to try. Made him want to say the things he had kept hidden for years.

"I've been running, too," he said quietly. "For a long time. Ever since my parents… betrayed me." He paused, glancing at her to see if she understood, but her expression remained calm, open, waiting. "They took everything from me. My savings, my future. And they didn't even care. They didn't even apologize. I've spent years trying to rebuild my life, but… I don't know. I guess I've never really gotten past it."

Meera didn't say anything right away. Her silence was comforting, though, like she was giving him the space to speak without judgment, without interruption.

"I don't trust people anymore," Aryan continued, his voice growing quieter. "I've kept everyone at a distance because... how can I trust anyone after that? How can I believe that anyone will ever really care about me if my own parents didn't?"

Meera's expression softened, and she nodded slowly, as if she understood. "Trust is fragile," she said quietly. "Once it's broken, it's hard to rebuild. But I think... I think sometimes we have to let people in, even if it's scary. Even if we've been hurt before."

Aryan stared at her, feeling a flicker of something—hope, maybe—stir inside him. "Is that what you're trying to do?" he asked, his voice low. "Are you trying to trust again?"

Meera's lips curved into a sad smile. "I don't know," she admitted. "I've spent so long trying to survive, trying to find my own way, that I don't know if I'm ready to trust anyone again. But I think... I think I want to try."

Aryan's felt squeezed. He wanted to try, too. For the first time in years, he felt like maybe—just maybe—he could open himself up to someone again. Maybe he could let down the walls he had built around himself, the walls that had kept him isolated for so long.

But he wasn't sure how. How do you trust again after everything has been broken? How do you believe in love, in loyalty, respect, when the people who were supposed to give you the most had let you down?

"Do you think it's possible?" Aryan asked, his voice barely a whisper. "Do you think we can ever really trust again?"

Meera looked at him then, her eyes soft and thoughtful. Her silence spoke volumes—a hesitation, a vulnerability that mirrored his own.

"I think we have to believe it's possible," she said finally. "Otherwise, what's the point of any of this?"

Aryan nodded, feeling the heaviness of her words settle over him. She was right. They had to believe. They had to try. Because if they didn't—if they let the pain of the past define them—then they would never be able to move forward. They would always be running, always trapped in the cycle of their own fear and loneliness.

But believing was easier said than done.

The train continued to rumble beneath them, the sound of the wheels on the tracks lulling the other passengers into sleep. But Aryan and Meera remained awake, both of them lost in their thoughts, both of them aware that something had shifted between them. They weren't just two strangers on a train anymore. They were two people who had opened up to each other, who had shared their pain, their fears, their hopes, though briefly.

And somehow, that made all the difference.

The rain began to slow, the steady patter against the windows growing softer, gentler. The storm was passing, though the clouds still lingered in the sky, heavy and dark. But for the first time since this journey began, Aryan felt a flicker of light—a glimmer of hope—that maybe, they were both on the path to something new.

Something real.

The Real Relationship

The night felt endless, the rain still fell steadily against the windows of the train, though it had softened to a gentle patter, as if the storm had finally begun to tire. Inside the coach, the dim lights shimmered, casting a faint glow over the sleeping passengers.

Aryan couldn't sleep. His mind was racing, tumbling over itself with thoughts he hadn't surfaced in years. Meera's words echoed in his head, stirring emotions he had long buried.

The conversation still lingered between them-the admissions, the vulnerability, the way they had connected over their shared sense of loss. They both knew there was more to say, but the words seemed caught in the tension of the moment, suspended like the rain outside that refused to fully stop.

"Relationships are strange," Aryan murmured, almost to himself.

He wasn't sure where the thought had come from, but now that it was out in the open, it felt like something worth exploring. Meera glanced at him; her eyes soft but alert.

"I mean… we spend so much time trying to figure them out, trying to make them work. But most of us don't even understand what a real relationship is."

Meera smiled softly, but it was a sad kind of smile. "Do any of us, really?" she asked. "We like to think we do, but the truth is, most relationships are built on expectations. And when those expectations aren't met, everything falls apart."

Aryan nodded, feeling the truth of her words settle over him like a heavy cloud. He thought about his own relationships—the failed friendships, the broken family ties, the connections that had never gone anywhere. They had all been built on expectations, hadn't they? He had expected his parents to support him, to be there for him when things got hard. He had expected love to be simple, easy. But life had a way of proving him wrong.

"Why do we even make them, then?" Aryan asked, more to himself than to her. "What makes a relationship real?"

Meera didn't answer right away. She seemed to be thinking, her fingers lightly tracing the edge of the window again. The silence between them felt reflective, not awkward, as though both were sifting through their own memories, their own experiences.

Finally, she sighed. "I think real relationships are made when we stop expecting everything to be perfect. When we stop thinking that the other person is going to complete us or fix us."

Meera continued, "a real relationship is built on accepting each other's flaws, on being willing to make the effort, day after day, even when it's hard."

Aryan thought about that for a moment. Was that where he had gone wrong? Had he expected too much from the people in his life? From his parents? From the family he had tried to love, but who had always slipped away? He had wanted so badly to be understood, to be accepted. But maybe, in his search for that connection, he had missed the point entirely.

"Do you think it's possible?" he asked quietly. "To build something real? Something that lasts?"

Meera turned to him then, her eyes meeting his. There was something raw in her gaze, something that made Aryan's heart skip a beat. "I don't know," she admitted, her voice barely above a whisper. "But I think... I think it's worth trying."

For a long time, neither of them spoke. The rain had slowed to a light drizzle, and the sound of the train moving steadily through the night filled the space between them. Aryan felt a strange sense of calm settle over him, even though he knew they had only scratched the surface of the conversation. There was so much more to say, so much more to listen.

Maybe that was the key to a real relationship, Aryan thought. Not expecting too much, too soon. Not trying to rush through the hard parts, or gloss over the imperfections. Maybe it was about letting things unfold naturally, in their own time, and being willing to stay, even when it wasn't easy.

Meera leaned back in her seat, her eyes drifting back to the window. Aryan watched her for a moment longer, feeling something shift inside him, something he hadn't felt in a long time.

Hope.

For the first time in years, he felt like maybe, just maybe, he could build something real. Not just with Meera, but with himself. He had to start there. He had to rebuild the relationship he had with himself before he could expect to connect with anyone else.

And maybe that's what this journey was really about. Not just running away from the past, but finding a way to move forward, to build something new. Something real.

The train continued its steady journey through the night, and for the first time, Aryan felt like he was no longer running. He was simply... moving. And maybe, that was enough.

The train rocked gently, the low hum of the engine a steady background noise as the night wore on. Most of the passengers were asleep now, wrapped in their thin blankets or leaning against the windows, their faces soft with the peacefulness that sleep brought. But Aryan and Meera remained awake, the depth of their conversation still hanging in the air between them.

"It's funny," Aryan said after a long silence. "We spend so much time thinking about how relationships should be, but we rarely ask ourselves why we even need them in the first place. Why do we make them? What's the point?"

Meera's gaze flicked toward him; her eyes thoughtful. "That's true," she said softly. "Maybe we're just afraid to be alone. Maybe that's why we keep trying, even when things fall apart. The idea of being alone is… unbearable, for most people."

Aryan nodded. He had always been afraid of being alone, though he would never admit it to anyone else. After the betrayal, after everything had been taken from him, he had isolated himself, thinking that if he cut everyone off, he wouldn't be hurt again. But the loneliness had crept in anyway, filling the spaces where love and trust should have been.

"I think you're right," Aryan said, his voice low. "But… I also think we make relationships because we need to believe in something bigger than ourselves. We need to believe that there's someone out there who can understand us, who can see us for who we really are, and still stay."

Meera's lips curved into a soft smile, though her eyes remained serious. "You think relationships are about being understood?"

"Partly," Aryan said, shrugging. "But I think they're also about growth. Real relationships push us to be better, to face our fears, to confront the things we've been running from. They force us to deal with our flaws, not just hide them. At least... that's what I think they should do."

Meera nodded slowly, as if considering his words. "Maybe that's why so many relationships fail," she said. "Because people don't want to do the hard work. They want the romance, the excitement, but they don't want to face the hard parts—the parts that make you question yourself."

Aryan leaned back in his seat, his mind swirling with thoughts. "You're right. People think relationships should be easy. They think love is enough. But it's not. It takes work—real work. Every day."

For a moment, they were both silent again, lost in their own thoughts. The rain had finally stopped, leaving the windows streaked with faint trails of water, but the air still smelled of wet earth and fresh beginnings. Aryan felt the pressure of the night pressing down on him, but it wasn't an unpleasant feeling. It was the kind of heaviness that came with clarity, with understanding.

"You know," Meera said quietly, her voice almost lost in the hum of the train, "I've always thought that real love wasn't about grand gestures or perfect moments.

It's about the little things. The small acts of kindness, the everyday effort to make the other person's life just a little bit easier."

Aryan nodded, feeling a strange sense of relief wash over him. That was it, wasn't it? The real relationship wasn't about the dramatic declarations of love, or the whirlwind romance that people always seemed to chase. It was about the everyday commitment to showing up, to being present, to putting in the effort even when it wasn't easy.

"It's like a partnership," Aryan said, echoing his thoughts from earlier. "You have to work together. It's not about one person always giving or one person always taking. It's about balance. It's about building something together, even when the world feels like it's falling apart."

Meera smiled softly, her fingers tracing the edge of the window again. The gesture had become familiar to Aryan now, and he found comfort in it, in the way she seemed to ground herself with such simple movements. "You sound like someone who's given this a lot of thought," she said, her voice teasing but gentle.

Aryan chuckled, though there was no humor in it. "Maybe," he admitted. "But that doesn't mean I've figured it out. I've failed more times than I can count. I've let people down. And I've been let down, too."

Meera's expression softened. There was a sadness in her eyes that mirrored his own. "We've all failed," she said quietly. "But I think the important thing is that we keep trying. Even when it's hard. Even when it feels impossible."

Aryan nodded, letting her words settle over him. He had spent so long running from his failures, from the broken relationships, from the people who had hurt him and perhaps from the people he had hurt in return. But maybe, just maybe, it was time to stop running.

"Do you think it's worth it?" Aryan asked, his voice barely above a whisper. "Do you think it's worth trying again, after everything?"

Meera was silent for a moment, her gaze drifting back to the window. The world outside was still dark, there was no hint of dawn to be seen. Yet there was a faint glow that barely touched the edges of the sky.

"I don't know," she said finally. "But I think… I think we have to believe it is. Otherwise, what's the point? How would we move on?"

Aryan stared at her, feeling a sense of awe wash over him. She was right. They had to believe it was worth it. They had to believe that something real could be built, even after all the pain, all the failures. Otherwise, they would spend the rest of their lives running, chasing something that didn't exist.

"Yeah," Aryan said softly. "I guess you're right."

The train continued its steady journey through the night, it was dark, yet one can see few lights break through the darkness. Aryan and Meera sat in silence, both of them feeling the heaviness of the conversation settle over them, both of them aware that something had shifted.

Maybe this was the beginning of something real. Something they had both been searching for, even if they hadn't known it.

Attraction – The Lack of it

The train hummed softly beneath them, a steady rhythm that seemed almost too calm for the storm of thoughts swirling in Aryan's mind. Outside, the night was endless, the darkness stretching far beyond what his eyes could perceive. But it wasn't the night outside that unsettled him—it was the conversation with Meera. Every word she had said earlier had lodged itself in his chest, stirring something he hadn't felt in years.

Attraction.

It was such a simple word, yet so complicated in meaning. It had always been a guiding force in Aryan's life, pulling him toward people, toward moments, like a magnet he couldn't resist. But sitting here, beside Meera, something felt different. The usual spark, the rush he had come to expect—it wasn't there. But that wasn't what troubled him. What troubled him was how much more there seemed to be beneath the surface. Something unspoken, a connection he didn't fully understand.

Aryan glanced at Meera. Her profile was illuminated by the dim light overhead, her face calm, yet distant. She had pulled back, just slightly, after their conversation, retreating into her own thoughts, and Aryan couldn't help but feel like she was hiding something. There was a mystery to her, something that went beyond her beauty or her quiet demeanor.

Who was she really? Why had she opened up to him so quickly, only to pull back as though guarding some unseen part of herself?

"Do you ever wonder," Aryan began, his voice barely above a whisper, "why we chase attraction so much? As if it's the only thing that matters?"

Meera didn't turn to face him immediately. Her fingers tapped lightly on the edge of her seat, a subtle, nervous gesture he hadn't noticed before. She took a long, slow breath, as if considering how to answer.

"Maybe because it's easier," she said softly. Her voice was calm, but there was something behind it—a hint of weariness, like she had seen too much of the world and had long ago grown tired of its illusions. "Attraction is simple. It's primal. It doesn't require thought or commitment. It just... happens."

Aryan leaned back, staring up at the ceiling of the train. The soft vibrations under his feet did nothing to calm the storm inside him. "And what happens when it fades? What's left after the attraction is gone?"

He hadn't meant to sound so desperate, but the question had come out that way, as though he were asking something far deeper than what he'd intended. As if the question wasn't about attraction at all, but about something much more personal.

Meera finally turned to him, her eyes catching the light in a way that made her expression unreadable. There was a pause, long enough for Aryan to feel the tension between them stretch thin, like a string pulled too tight. "When the spark fades," she began, her voice low and almost… haunted, "you have to decide if you're willing to stay. But most people… they run. They chase that thrill somewhere else. Because staying means facing things you might not be ready for."

Aryan's pulse quickened. There was something about the way she said it—something hidden in her words, as if she wasn't just talking about attraction, but about her own life. Her own choices. Her own fears.

"You sound like you've run before," Aryan said carefully, watching her closely. Her expression didn't change, but there was a flicker in her eyes—just for a second—that told him he had hit something raw.

Meera turned back toward the window, her reflection staring back at her from the glass, the rain-soaked darkness outside creating a mirror of the person she was trying to hide. "We all run," she said after a long pause. "Some of us run from the past. Some of us run from the future. And some of us…" she hesitated, her voice trailing off. "Some of us run from ourselves."

Aryan's heart tightened. The way she said it, the look on her face—it was as if she was speaking directly to him, even though her words were veiled in mystery. He had run too, hadn't he? From the pain, from the betrayal, from the fear of trusting someone again. And now, sitting beside Meera, he couldn't help but wonder if they were both running in the same direction—away from the truth.

"What are you running from?" Aryan asked, his voice barely above a whisper, though the strain of the question hung heavy in the air.

Meera didn't answer right away. The silence between them was thick, oppressive, as though the entire train had gone still just to hear what she would say. When she finally spoke, her voice was so quiet Aryan had to strain to hear it.

"Everything," she said. And then, without looking at him, she added, "But mostly… myself."

Aryan's breath caught in his throat. He wanted to ask her more, wanted to pull back the layers she had so carefully wrapped around herself, but he didn't know how. He didn't know if he had the right.

"I've been attracted to people before," Aryan said, breaking the tension with a shift in the conversation. "But it never lasted. The attraction always fades, and then you're left wondering what's real. If anything, ever was."

Meera's lips curved into a small, sad smile. "Maybe that's the problem. We confuse attraction with love. We think they're the same thing, but they're not."

Aryan's pulse raced. There was more to her words—something deeper, something she wasn't saying outright. "And what happens when you realize the attraction isn't enough? What do you do then?"

Meera turned to him, her gaze piercing. Her eyes were dark and unreadable, as though she was looking straight through him. "You either walk away, or you stay and face the truth. But most people don't stay. It's too hard. Too painful."

Aryan's heart pounded in his chest. He felt the ++++ of her words pressing down on him, as though she were speaking from experience—from something she hadn't told him yet. And suddenly, he wanted to know. He wanted to know everything. Who was she? What had she been through? What was she running from?

"Why didn't you run?" Aryan asked, his voice steady but laced with curiosity. "Why are you here, on this train, sitting next to me, talking about things that most people would never admit?"

Meera looked away, her eyes clouding with something Aryan couldn't quite place. When she spoke, her voice was low, almost hollow. "Maybe I'm still running. But maybe… I'm just tired of being alone."

The words hung in the air, heavy and full of unspoken emotion. Aryan felt a chill run through him, not from the cold, but from the realization that they were both searching for the same thing, even if neither of them could fully admit it.

The train continued to move, its steady hum filling the silence between them. And yet, despite the calmness of the night, there was an undeniable tension in the air—a mystery neither of them had yet unraveled, but both could feel.

Maybe it wasn't just about attraction. Maybe it was about facing the truth of who they were, about staying when everything inside them wanted to run.

And maybe, just maybe, they weren't so different after all.

The train continued its journey through the night, but Aryan was wide awake. His conversation with Meera had stirred something in him, something that had been buried for years under layers of loneliness and guardedness. He had always believed that relationships were complicated, that people were fickle, but now, sitting beside her, he began to wonder if maybe he had been focusing on the wrong things all along.

The train's steady hum seemed louder now, as if amplifying the thoughts running through Aryan's mind. The conversation had turned heavy, burdened with the truths neither of them had fully spoken.

Attraction—it was supposed to be simple, easy. But sitting here with Meera, Aryan was beginning to realize just how much damage it could do when it was misunderstood.

"It's like chasing shadows," Aryan murmured, his voice low, more to himself than to Meera. "You think it's something real, something you can hold onto, but the closer you get, the more it slips away."

Meera remained quiet; her gaze distant as she stared out the window. The faint reflection of her face in the glass was ghostly, and Aryan could see the way her jaw clenched, the way her hands rested tensely in her lap. She wasn't just thinking about his words; she was living them. Reliving them, perhaps.

"Attraction can hurt," she said, breaking the silence. Her voice was soft, almost fragile, as if she were trying to hold back something deeper. "It can make you believe in something that was never there. It fools you into thinking you're connected to someone, that they see you, really see you. But when it fades..." She paused, exhaling slowly. "When it fades, you're left wondering if you were ever really seen at all."

Aryan felt a chill run down his spine. He knew exactly what she meant. He had been there lost in the allure of someone's presence, someone's persona, only to realize too late that what he felt wasn't real. The connection he thought he had was a lie, a projection of his own desires onto someone who couldn't, or wouldn't, reciprocate.

"Attraction can be a lie," Aryan agreed, his voice tight. "It tricks you into thinking you're closer to someone than you are. You tell yourself it's love, perhaps, and that it's real. But sometimes, it's just... a distraction. Something that keeps you from seeing the truth."

Meera's hands tightened slightly, her knuckles turning white against her skin. "It's worse when you don't realize it right away," she said. Her tone was darker now, almost bitter. "When you spend months, years even, believing that what you feel is mutual, only to find out later that you were just convenient. That they were never really attracted to you, but to the idea of you."

Aryan looked at her, seeing the rawness in her eyes, the pain she was trying to keep at bay. She was speaking from experience, from wounds that had yet to fully heal. He wanted to ask, wanted to know who had hurt her like this, but something held him back.

"Was it someone you loved?" Aryan asked carefully, his voice gentle, afraid of pushing too far.

Meera's gaze dropped, her eyes flickering with a sadness that seemed to pull the warmth from the air around them. "I never knew what love meant," she said, her voice barely above a whisper. "Never knew if love even existed… it was all wrong. He wasn't in love with me. He was in love with himself, and how he can control me."

Aryan's felt a vacuum in his heart. He had felt that sting before—the realization that you had meant far less to someone than they had meant to you. "And when that feeling faded," he said softly, "you were left out."

Meera nodded; her lips pressed into a thin line. "May be, the attraction was never there. And just like that, it was over."

A heavy silence fell between them, their shared confession created an unspoken tension in the air. Aryan knew that feeling all too well—the sudden, brutal end of something that had felt so important, so real, only to realize it had been fragile, built on nothing but fleeting desire.

"It's like being discarded," Aryan said, his voice low. "Like you were never more than a passing moment in someone's life, and once that moment was over, they moved on without a second thought."

Meera glanced at him, her eyes filled with a mixture of understanding and sorrow. "Exactly," she whispered. "You start questioning everything. Was any of it real? Did I imagine it all? Did I mean anything?"

The rawness in her voice cut through Aryan, and for a moment, he didn't know what to say. What could he say? He had felt the same doubts, the same bitter questions gnawing at him after his own experiences. The pain of being discarded, of feeling like you were nothing more than a phase in someone's life, had left scars on his heart that still ached when he thought about them.

"It makes you doubt yourself," Aryan said after a long pause. "You start wondering if you're even worthy of being loved, or if you're just someone people get bored of."

Meera turned her head slowly, her eyes locking onto his, and Aryan felt a shiver run through him. There was something in her gaze, something deep and unspoken that felt like a mirror of his own fears.

"I think that's what hurt the most," Meera said softly. "It's not about losing him, but losing myself. I couldn't recognize who I was anymore. I stopped living and became an existence. I did what he wanted and for his approval. And when it was gone, I was left nothing."

Aryan's heart clenched. He knew that feeling all too well—the loss of identity, the way a failed relationship could strip away the parts of yourself that you had once taken for granted. "It's easy to lose ourself for someone else," Aryan said quietly. "You start believing that they're the answer to everything, and when it is over, you're left with a version of yourself you don't even recognize."

Meera smiled sadly, her eyes reflecting a pain that Aryan felt mirrored inside him. "It makes you question everything," she said. "It makes you wonder if you were ever enough. If you'll ever be enough."

The vulnerability in her words struck Aryan harder than he expected. He had never imagined that someone like Meera—so composed, so seemingly self-assured—could harbor the same insecurities that plagued him. It made him realize just how fragile people really were, how easily they could be broken by something as simple as misplaced attraction.

"It's not about being enough," Aryan said after a moment, his voice soft but firm. "It's about finding someone who sees you—really sees you—and doesn't need you to be anything other than who you are."

Meera looked at him then, her eyes wide with something close to surprise. For a moment, neither of them spoke, but the silence was different now. It wasn't heavy with pain or regret. It was filled with something else, something fragile but hopeful.

"Maybe that's what we're all looking for," Meera said softly. "Someone who sees us for who we are, not who they want us to be."

Aryan nodded slowly, allowing the pressure of her words settle over him. "Yeah," he said quietly. "Maybe that's the only kind of attraction that matters."

The train rattled gently as it pushed through the darkness, but inside the coach, everything felt still. Aryan's mind was racing, feeling the burden of the conversation he and Meera were having—one he hadn't expected but couldn't stop himself from diving deeper into. It wasn't just about attraction anymore; it was about connection, about seeing someone beyond the surface, and the devastating consequences when that vision blurred into something less.

Meera hadn't said anything in a while, but her presence beside him was enough to keep his thoughts moving. She was different from anyone he'd ever met, not just because of the way she spoke about pain and attraction with such honesty, but because of the way she carried it—like a burden she had learned to bear without letting it crush her completely.

"Do you ever think," Aryan began, his voice quiet, "that maybe we're looking for something impossible? That the kind of attraction we want, the kind of connection we need, doesn't exist?"

Meera turned her head slightly, her eyes catching the faint light as she considered his words. There was a sadness in her expression, something that told Aryan she had asked herself the same question more times than she cared to admit.

"I used to think it existed," Meera said softly, her voice tinged with the weariness of someone who never loved yet lost. "I used to believe in soul mates, in the idea that there's one person out there who's meant for you. Someone who completes you, who sees every part of you, and still loves you. But now..."

She trailed off, staring out into the dark night beyond the window, her reflection mingling with the rain-splattered glass. Her silence spoke volumes. A quite intensity lingered in her motionless form.

"I think maybe we've been sold a lie," Meera continued, her voice quieter now, as if speaking aloud was an admission she wasn't sure she was ready to make. "This idea of perfect love, of perfect attraction. It's not real. We're just people. Imperfect, messy, and broken. And maybe no one ever really sees all of us."

Aryan had felt that exact same disillusionment before but hearing it from Meera somehow made it more real, more final. "It's hard to accept, isn't it?" Aryan said. "The idea that maybe we'll never find that kind of connection. That we'll always be a little bit alone."

Meera's eyes wavered, betraying her uncertainty and for the first time that night, Aryan saw something crack in her—a vulnerability she hadn't shown before. "Maybe that's the hardest part," she whispered. "The loneliness. Even when you're with someone, you can still feel it. You can still feel the distance. You can still be alone."

Aryan exhaled slowly, feeling the truth of her words wash over him. He had been there sitting beside someone, holding their hand, but feeling like they were miles away. Like the attraction that had once pulled them together was suddenly meaningless, incapable of bridging the growing gap between them.

"I think I've been afraid of that," Aryan admitted, his voice low, almost hesitant. "Afraid that no matter how much I care about someone, no matter how attracted I am to them, it'll never be enough to close the distance. I'll always feel… separate. Alone."

Meera's gaze softened, and Aryan saw a flicker of understanding in her eyes. "It's not just you," she said gently. "We all feel that way, I think. Attraction can bring you together, but it's not enough to keep you there. And when it fades, that's when the loneliness creeps in."

They sat in silence for a while, the gentle rocking of the train the only sound between them. The night outside seemed endless, an infinite stretch of darkness, but Aryan felt like he was standing on the edge of something—something deeper, more profound. He wasn't sure what it was yet, but he could feel it pulling him forward, urging him to keep going.

"Maybe that's why we keep chasing it," Aryan said after a long pause. "Attraction. Even when we know it won't last, even when we know it might hurt us in the end, we still want it. Because for a moment, it makes us feel seen. It makes us feel like we matter."

Meera turned to him; her eyes filled with a quiet intensity that made Aryan's breath catch in his throat. "But it's dangerous, isn't it".

The train's movement felt almost hypnotic now, the rhythm of the tracks beneath them matching the pulse of thoughts racing through Aryan's mind. He couldn't stop thinking about what Meera had said—about being discarded, about losing herself in someone who never really saw her and it can be dangerous. It mirrored his own pain so closely that it was almost unnerving, like looking into a reflection of his own heartache.

For a long moment, neither of them spoke. The silence between them was comfortable now, not filled with tension, but with an understanding that didn't need words. Aryan glanced at Meera, catching the way her eyes had softened, as if some of the weight she carried had lightened ever so slightly.

"It's strange, isn't it?" Aryan finally said, breaking the silence. "How we can give so much of ourselves to someone who never really sees us. And then, when they're gone, we're left trying to put ourselves back together."

Meera sighed softly, her gaze drifting back to the window. "It's more than strange," she said quietly. "It's terrifying. You think you're building something real, something that matters, but then one day you wake up and realize it was never about you at all. It was about what they wanted from you."

Aryan nodded, feeling the truth of her words sink into him. He had felt that same terror, the realization that all the effort, all the love, had been one-sided. "And when the attraction fades," he added, "it's like everything you built crumbles into nothing."

Meera was silent for a moment, but Aryan could feel her agreement in the way her shoulders tensed slightly, the way her fingers absentmindedly traced the edge of her seat. "That's why it hurts so much," she said after a pause. "Because you've given so much of yourself, and then you're left wondering if any of it was real."

Aryan knew that feeling—the emptiness, the sense of betrayal not just by the other person, but by your own emotions. You question everything, every moment, every feeling. Was it all just an illusion? Was it all a lie?

"Attraction can be deceiving," Aryan said, his voice low but steady. "It makes you believe in something that's not really there. It makes you think you've found a connection, but it's just a trick—a trick your heart plays on you."

Meera looked at him then, her eyes dark and filled with something unspoken, something Aryan couldn't quite place. "But what if it's not just attraction?" she asked softly. "What if it's something deeper? Something real, but we're too afraid to recognize it because we've been hurt before?"

Her words hung in the air between them, heavy with meaning. Aryan felt his pulse quicken. Was that what this was? Was that what had been happening between them all along? He had been so focused on understanding the nature of attraction, on trying to figure out why it always seemed to fail him, that he hadn't stopped to consider the possibility that maybe, just maybe, what he was feeling now was something else.

Something real.

He didn't know what to say. The idea that this—whatever was happening between him and Meera—could be more than just a fleeting connection, more than just a moment shared between two strangers, was both terrifying and exhilarating.

"What if we're just scared?" Aryan asked quietly, voicing the thought that had been gnawing at him since their conversation had begun. "What if we've been so hurt, so burned by past relationships, that we can't even recognize something real when it's right in front of us?"

Meera's gaze softened, but she didn't respond right away. The silence between them deepened, the train's steady hum filling the space. Aryan could feel the pressure of the question pressing down on both of them, heavy and unrelenting. It wasn't just about attraction anymore. It was about trust. It was about believing that something deeper could exist after everything they had been through.

"Maybe," Meera said finally, her voice so soft Aryan almost didn't hear her. "Maybe we're both too scared to see what's real because we've been hurt so many times before. Maybe it's easier to think it's just attraction because if we let ourselves believe in something more…"

She trailed off, but Aryan understood exactly what she meant. If they let themselves believe it was more, if they opened themselves up to the possibility that this connection between them was something real, then they were also opening themselves up to the possibility of getting hurt again. Of being vulnerable in ways, they hadn't been in a long time.

"It's a risk," Aryan said quietly, more like a self-talk. "Letting yourself feel again after everything. It's a risk I'm not sure I know how to take anymore."

Meera's eyes glisted with something close to sadness, but also understanding. "Me either," she admitted. "But I think... I think maybe that's the point. Maybe we're supposed to be scared. Maybe if it didn't scare us, it wouldn't be real."

Aryan stared at her, feeling his heart race in a way that had nothing to do with fear and everything to do with hope. Hope that maybe, just maybe, this was more than what he had first thought. Maybe the connection he felt with Meera wasn't just attraction. Maybe it was something deeper. Something worth risking.

But even as the thought crossed his mind, doubt crept in. How could, he be sure? How could he trust that this time, it wouldn't end the same way? That he wouldn't end up broken again, left questioning everything, just like before?

"How do you know?" Aryan asked softly, his voice almost trembling with the heaviness of the question. "How do you know when it's real?"

Meera smiled then, a small, sad smile that didn't quite reach her eyes. "I don't think you ever really know," she said quietly. "Not until it's too late."

Aryan's heart sank. The honesty in her words, the rawness of her truth, felt like a blow to his chest. She was right. There were no guarantees, no way to know for sure if what they were feeling was real, or if it was just another illusion, another trick their hearts were playing on them.

"But maybe that's the risk," Meera continued, her voice soft but steady. "Maybe the only way to know is to take the chance. To believe that maybe this time… it's different."

Aryan's breath caught in his throat. Different. Could it be? Could this be the moment that changed everything? He didn't know. But as he looked at Meera, at the way her eyes held a mixture of fear and hope, he felt something shift inside him.

Perhaps, it was worth the risk.

The train continued its steady journey through the night, the rhythmic sound of the wheels on the tracks filling the space between them. For a while, neither Aryan nor Meera spoke, but the silence wasn't uncomfortable. It was as though both of them were lost in their own thoughts, processing everything they had just shared.

Aryan leaned back in his seat, staring out the window into the darkness beyond. Meera's words echoed in his mind—the fear of trusting again, the risk of letting yourself feel something real after being hurt so many times. He had been running from that fear for years, convincing himself that attraction was enough, that he didn't need anything deeper.

But sitting here with Meera, something had changed. It wasn't just about attraction anymore. It wasn't about the spark or the excitement that came with meeting someone new. It was about something else—something quieter, more profound. The connection they shared wasn't based on fleeting desire or surface-level chemistry. It was based on the simple fact that they understood each other in ways that no one else had.

But even as Aryan felt that connection deepen, the fear lingered.

What if it wasn't real? What if this was just another illusion, another trick that would end in heartbreak? He wasn't sure if he was ready to take that risk. He wasn't sure if he could.

"I think..." Meera's voice broke the silence, soft but certain. "I think sometimes we have to stop asking ourselves if it's real. Maybe we'll never know for sure. Maybe the only thing we can do is let go of the fear and see what happens."

Aryan turned to her; her face illuminated by the faint glow of the overhead light. There was something in her expression that calmed him, something that made him believe, even if only for a moment, that maybe she was right.

"Let go of the fear," Aryan repeated softly, as if testing the words on his tongue. Could he do that? Could he really let go of the fear that had kept him from opening up for so long?

Meera nodded, her eyes meeting his. "Maybe it's not about being sure. Maybe it's just about being willing to try."

Aryan's heart raced. Willing to try. He wasn't sure if he had the strength to try again, to risk the pain and disappointment that had followed him like a shadow for years. But something about Meera's presence, about the way she spoke, made him feel as though maybe—it was worth it.

"Do you think it's possible?" Aryan asked, his voice quiet. "To let go of the past, to stop running?"

Meera smiled softly, though it was tinged with sadness. "I think it's possible," she said. "But I don't think it's easy. Maybe that's why we're both here—on this train. Maybe we're trying to figure out how to stop running."

Aryan's breath become hollow. She was right. They had both been running—running from the past, from the pain, from the fear of being hurt again. But here, in this quiet space between them, he felt a flicker of hope that maybe they didn't have to run anymore.

Maybe this was the beginning of something new. Something real.

The train jerked slightly as it crossed a bend in the tracks, and Aryan felt himself shift in his seat, pulling him back into the moment. Meera was watching him closely, her eyes filled with a mixture of curiosity and something else—something unspoken but undeniable.

"I guess we'll see what happens," Aryan said finally, a small smile tugging at the corners of his lips. The fear hadn't disappeared, but it felt lighter now, less overwhelming. Maybe he didn't have to know all the answers right now. Maybe it was enough to just be here, in this moment, with Meera.

Meera returned his smile, her expression softening. "Yeah," she said quietly. "Maybe we will."

For the first time in what felt like years, Aryan felt a sense of peace settle over him. The uncertainty was still there, but it no longer felt like a load pressing down on him. It felt like an opportunity—a chance to stop running, to stop hiding behind the walls he had built around himself.

The night outside was still dark, but somewhere on the horizon, Aryan could sense the faintest glimmer of dawn. It wasn't visible yet, but he knew it was coming. And this may be the start of something new, perhaps, something real.

The Oppressor is the Oppressed

The darkness outside the train window mirrored the turmoil inside Meera's heart. For years, she had lived in the shadow of someone else's expectations, imprisoned not by bars but by the chains of emotional manipulation. The man who never loved—the man she had never trusted to build a life with—had turned into her oppressor. But what hurt the most wasn't the oppression itself; it was the realization that somewhere along the way, she had become complicit in her own suffering.

Her fingers trembled as she traced the cool glass of the window, lost in thought. Aryan's words echoed in her mind, pulling her deeper into memories she had tried so hard to forget. But tonight, under the cover of the stormy sky, Meera couldn't escape them anymore.

How I wish I could take you away from all of this. These were words she had whispered to herself in the dead of night, words she had never dared to say aloud. For years, she had been surrounded by people who stole her dreams, who convinced her that she had no right to want anything more. Dream stealers, she called them. They manipulated her gracious nature, twisted her love into obedience, and wore her down until the lines between what she wanted and what they demanded blurred beyond recognition.

Her husband had been the worst of them.

He had seemed fine to others—charming, kind, and attentive. But as time went on, the charm faded, replaced by control, possessiveness, and subtle cruelty. It didn't happen all at once. No, it was gradual, insidious. It was in the small things—his disapproving looks when she spoke too freely, the way he dismissed her dreams, his insistence that her role was to support him, not herself.

At first, she resisted. She had always been strong-willed, determined to live the life she had imagined for herself. But over time, his words began to creep into her mind, taking root like weeds in a garden. He never told her outright that she couldn't dream, that she couldn't be anything more than what he wanted her to be. But the message was clear.

She had allowed it to happen, hadn't she? That was the part that cut the deepest. She had let herself be oppressed.

How I want you to live the life you deserve—away from all those people who have snatched you from yourself. Meera's breath hitched as she replayed these thoughts over and over. How had it come to this? How had she, a woman who once believed in the power of her own voice, allowed herself to be silenced?

The worst part wasn't his cruelty; it was the fact that he made her question her own worth. He made her doubt every thought, every decision, every feeling. And somehow, without even realizing it, she had started to believe him. She had started to believe that she wasn't enough.

It wasn't just him who had held her back. It was the entire world she had built around herself—a world full of people who expected her to fit into their mold, to be the version of herself that was convenient for them. But her husband had been the master of that world, and she had become his willing prisoner.

But tonight, as the train rattled on into the unknown, Meera felt something shift inside her. She had survived it, hadn't she? She had endured years of being told that she was too much, or too little, or simply not enough. But she had also found a way to fight back. She had found a way to dream again.

No, I don't want you to leave anyone, she had often thought. I want you to stand your ground. For too long, Meera had equated obedience with fate, submission with safety. She had allowed herself to believe that to be obedient to someone meant to sacrifice her own happiness. But now, as she sat beside Aryan, her thoughts spiraling deeper into the past, she realized how wrong she had been.

Her husband wasn't just her oppressor—he was oppressed, too.

He was trapped in his own prison, one made of fear and insecurity. He didn't control her because he wanted to; he controlled her because he didn't know any other way to feel powerful. His dominance over her was a reflection of his own helplessness. And that was the tragic irony of it all.

The oppressor was the oppressed.

Meera had thought of leaving him, of escaping the life that had suffocated her. But she had stayed, not because of loyalty, love or her children, but because she never knew how to escape. She looked towards God, prayed for years for a sign, and when she saw the sign, she gathered all the courage she had and walked out of the pain, the fear, the humiliation that drove her insane for years. And in some twisted way, she had felt responsible, for allowing herself to be oppressed.

But not anymore.

The dictionary definition of oppression: the state of being subject to unjust treatment or control. Mostly, people think of an oppressor as someone else—someone outside of ourselves. But sometimes, the oppressor is within.

As Meera sat in the dimly lit train, listening to the steady rhythm of the wheels on the tracks, she began to understand something she hadn't allowed herself to fully acknowledge before. She had been her own oppressor.

Her husband had held her down, yes, but she had played a part in her own suffering. She had allowed his words to define her, to make her feel small. She had stayed, not because she had no choice, but because she had convinced herself that she didn't deserve more.

But that had changed. She had changed.

The oppression was gradual, unfolding over years, each moment of doubt building upon the last. It wasn't until Meera began to see herself clearly that she understood just how deeply she had been oppressed—not just by him, but by her own fears.

She had feared freedom. The thought of living her own life, of standing up for herself, had terrified her more than staying in a loveless, controlling marriage. To leave him, to demand more, would have required her to face herself, to confront the image of the woman she had become.

And that had been the hardest part.

Freedom was terrifying, but it was also the only way forward. To break free, Meera knew she had to reject the version of herself that had been shaped by years of manipulation. She had to break down the walls she had built around her heart, walls that had kept her safe but also trapped.

The oppressor is the oppressed. Meera repeated the words in her mind, feeling their pressure settle into her bones. She wasn't just the victim of her husband's control. She had been her own jailer, her own worst enemy.

But now, she was ready to change. She was ready to break free.

Meera had always wondered how she had let it happen—how she had allowed herself to be reduced to someone she no longer recognized. The woman she saw in the mirror each morning was a stranger to her now. Gone was the vibrant, ambitious woman who had once believed she could change the world. In her place stood a shell, hollowed out by years of living under someone else's control. But as much as it pained her to admit, it hadn't all been his doing.

The realization stung, but it was inescapable: She had given him that power. At first, it was easy to make excuses. Perhaps he was under stress, dealing with things that weighed on him. He never loved her, but he had a temper. "It's just his way," she had told herself countless times. The justifications came so naturally that she hardly noticed when they started to chip away at her sense of self. Each excuse was a small act of surrender—an admission that her feelings, her needs, were somehow less important than his.

And the worst part? She believed it. She had let herself believe that his anger, his control, his dismissiveness—none of it was his fault. It was the world, the pressures of life, his upbringing. Anything but the truth.

It wasn't always the yelling, the harsh words or the beatings that broke her down, though there had been plenty of that. Sometimes, it was the silence. The cold, impenetrable wall he built around himself, shutting her out without a word. She would try to talk to him, to bridge the gap that had grown between them, but his eyes were always distant, his responses clipped and dismissive.

"You're not doing enough."

"Can't you do more?"

Those words had been like poison, sinking into her skin, seeping into her bones. Over time, they had become a part of her, a narrative she repeated to herself whenever she felt upset, whenever she questioned her own worth.

"Maybe I am too sensitive."

"Maybe it's me."

But deep down, Meera knew the truth. It wasn't her. She had always been someone who felt deeply, who loved deeply. But in the wrong hands, that kind of heart can be a weapon used against you.

And her husband—the man she expected nothing — had wielded that weapon with precision.

The first time she realized she needed to leave was after a particularly bad argument. He had lashed out, as he always did, accusing her of things she hadn't done, blaming her for his own frustrations. But this time, something shifted inside her. Instead of crying, instead of apologizing as she had so many times before, she stood there, silent, watching him.

And in that moment, she saw him clearly—for the first time in years. He wasn't the towering figure she had once feared, nor was he the invincible force she had built him up to be in her mind. He was a man—just a man—filled with insecurities, lashing out because he couldn't bear to face his own failures. And she was more than what he could see.

He was scared. Scared of losing control, scared of being seen for who he really was—vulnerable, fragile, human. As it is said, " a weak man cannot handle a strong woman, he would never know what to do with her."

For years, he had projected that fear onto her, using her as a mirror to reflect the things he hated about himself. And for years, she had absorbed it, internalizing his anger, his disappointment, as if it were her own.

But not anymore.

The hardest part wasn't leaving him. It wasn't packing her bags, walking out the door, and starting over. The hardest part was forgiving herself.

For years, she had stayed. She had told herself that things would get better, that he would change, that if he just loved her a little, he would finally see her. But he never did. And she had spent too long hoping, too long waiting for a version of him that didn't exist.

She had stayed because she was afraid. Afraid of being alone, afraid of starting over, afraid that maybe she didn't deserve more. But in staying, she had lost herself.

Reclaiming herself, that was the real battle.

She had started small. A conversation with a friend, a long walk by herself, a quiet moment in the mirror where she didn't turn away from her reflection. She had begun to remember the things that made her who she was before him. The things she loved; the things that made her feel alive.

It wasn't easy. Every step felt like a mountain, every decision weighed down by the years of doubt and guilt that still clung to her like a second skin. But with each passing day, she grew stronger. She started to hear her own voice again, faint at first, but growing louder with every moment of clarity.

The journey wasn't over. Far from it. But now, for the first time in a long time, she could see the road ahead. And she knew—no matter how long it took, no matter how difficult it was—she wouldn't be walking it alone. She had herself now.

The oppressor is the oppressed. Meera understood that now. Her husband had been as trapped as she was—trapped by his fears, by his insecurities, by the things he refused to face. But that didn't absolve him of the pain he had caused her. It didn't excuse the years of torment, the nights she spent crying in silence, the moments she felt like she was disappearing into nothingness.

But it did give her clarity. It gave her strength.

Because now, as she sat on this train, moving forward for the first time in years, she realized something powerful. She had survived. She had come out the other side of the storm, battered but not broken. And that, in itself, was a victory.

She wasn't the woman she once was. She was something more—something stronger, something wiser. She had been forged in the fires of her pain, and though it had left scars, it had also made her unbreakable.

It was the hardest truth to accept. Harder than the years of control, harder than the manipulation, harder even than the nights of loneliness spent in a marriage that had never felt like home.

He had never loved her.

Meera had spent years convincing herself otherwise, longing for moments of tenderness—the rare, fleeting glimpses of the man she would want to fall in love with. But now, in the silence of this train journey, with the space to breathe and reflect, she saw the truth clearly.

It wasn't love. It had never been loving.

It had been control. It had been possession, rather ruling. It had been needing, but not the kind of need born out of affection or care. It was the need to dominate, to shape her into something that fit into his world, to keep her small enough so that he could feel big.

Love doesn't shrink you, she realized. Love doesn't make you feel like less.

The signs had been there from the beginning, but like so many people in the throes of new life, Meera had ignored them. He portrayed his jealousy as protectiveness, his need to know her every move for devotion. She had told herself that the way he questioned her relations, the way he discouraged her ambitions, was just his way of being normal.

But normal is not caring and it doesn't suffocate.

Care doesn't make you feel like you have to choose between your dreams and your relationship. Care doesn't isolate you from the people who once made you feel alive. Care is understood.

But that's what had happened. Slowly, so slowly that Meera hadn't even noticed it at first, he had cut her off from everything that gave her joy. Her friends, her family, her books—they had all been sacrificed on the altar of his insecurities.

And she had let it happen. She had let herself believe that this was normal or just fate.

The realization hit her like a cold wave. He hadn't loved her. Not in the way she needed, not in the way that mattered. His love, if it could even be called that, was conditional—dependent on her fitting into the narrow role he had carved out for her.

And she had tried. God, how she had tried. She had bent and folded herself into the version of a woman she thought he wanted, cutting away pieces of herself in the process. Each compromise, each sacrifice, had been a small death, a little piece of her soul fading into the background.

But it had never been enough.

No matter how much of herself she gave up, no matter how hard she worked to be the woman he demanded, he was never satisfied. There was always something else—some new flaw to point out, some new expectation to meet.

That was the thing about him. He didn't want love. He wanted control. He wanted someone who would bend to his will, someone who would validate his insecurities by making herself smaller, quieter, more obedient.

And for a long time, Meera had done just that. She had shrunk herself down to fit into his world, telling herself that this was what love required. That love meant sacrifice, that it meant putting someone else's needs ahead of your own.

But now, sitting in the quiet of the train, with the gravity of the past pressing down on her, she realized how wrong she had been.

Love doesn't demand that you lose yourself.

Love doesn't ask you to give up the things that make you who you are. It doesn't ask you to silence your voice, to dim your light, to make yourself smaller so that someone else can feel big.

Love, real love, builds you up. It makes you feel seen, understood, valued. It makes you feel like more, not less.

And that's what had been missing all along.

Her husband had never truly seen her—not for who she really was. He had only ever seen the version of her that served his needs, the version that fit neatly into the life he wanted to create for himself.

He had never asked about her. He had never asked about her dreams. He had never cared about the things that made her feel alive, the passions that fueled her soul. In fact, he had dismissed them, mocked them, made her feel foolish for wanting more than what he could offer.

And for a time, she had believed him. She had allowed herself to believe that her dreams were too big, too unrealistic, too foolish. She had allowed his voice to drown out her own, until she could no longer hear the whisper of her own desires.

But now, she could hear it again. That voice, faint but growing stronger with each passing moment.

It told her that she was worthy of more. That she deserved to be loved—not for what she could give, not for how well she could fit into someone else's life, but for who she was.

For who she truly was.

The pain of the realization was sharp, cutting through her like a blade. To know that she had given so much of herself to someone who had never truly loved her—that was a wound that would take time to heal.

But with the pain came clarity. And with clarity came strength.

She was no longer the woman who believed she had to earn love by making herself smaller. She was no longer the woman who would sacrifice her own happiness for someone else's approval.

She had survived.

And more than that, she had found herself again.

Love is not control. Love is not possession. Love does not demand that you give up your dreams, your voice, your identity.

Her husband had never loved her. But that didn't mean she was unworthy of love. It didn't mean she had failed.

If anything, it meant she had survived something far more damaging than a loveless marriage—she had survived losing herself. And now, she had the chance to reclaim everything she had given up.

She wasn't a victim of his lack of love. She was a survivor of her own journey to self-discovery.

The oppressor may have been oppressed by his own fears, his own insecurities, but Meera was no longer bound by them. She had broken free. And with that freedom came the knowledge that she was capable of more—more love, more happiness, more life.

She would never settle for anything less again.

The train began to slow, its steady rhythm gradually fading into a gentle hum, and Meera could feel the shift inside herself as clearly as she could feel the slowing of the train. The past had held her captive for so long—the pain, the fear, the lies she had told herself. But now, something had changed. Something had broken free inside her.

It wasn't a sudden revelation. It was a quiet truth, something that had been building inside her over time, slowly taking shape in the darkest corners of her mind. She had always known it was there, lurking just beneath the surface, waiting for her to acknowledge it.

She had been oppressed. Not just by her husband, but by her own silence. By her willingness to accept less than she deserved. But now, as she sat in the dimly lit train car, watching the shadows of the past fall away, she realized that the oppression was over.

She had freed herself.

It hadn't been easy, and it wouldn't be easy going forward. But Meera understood now that the hardest part wasn't leaving. It wasn't even confronting the years of emotional abuse, the manipulation, the way her husband had twisted life into something unrecognizable.

The hardest part was forgiving herself. Forgiving herself for staying as long as she had, for believing that his version of love was all she was worthy of.

But she had learned something powerful through the process—something that would stay with her for the rest of her life.

She wasn't weak. She wasn't foolish or naive. She was strong. It took strength to endure what she had endured. It took strength to stay when everything inside her was breaking. But it also took strength to leave. To choose herself, after so many years of choosing him.

She wasn't just a survivor of her marriage. She was a survivor of herself.

The night outside the train window seemed softer now, the darkness no longer oppressive, but comforting. The journey wasn't over—not by a long shot—but for the first time in years, Meera felt like she was truly moving forward. Not just physically, but emotionally, mentally. She had taken the first step in reclaiming her life; in rediscovering the woman she had been before her husband had worn her down.

But she wasn't looking back at the woman she once was. She was looking forward—to the woman she was becoming. Someone stronger. Someone wiser.

There was still pain, of course. The scars her husband had left on her heart would take time to heal. But she wasn't afraid of that pain anymore. She wasn't afraid to face it, to feel it. Because now, she knew that the pain didn't define her. It didn't control her.

She controlled herself.

The oppressor had been oppressed by his own demons. His fear of losing control had turned him into someone cruel, someone desperate to hold power over her. But she would no longer be bound by his insecurities. She would no longer be defined by the way he saw her.

She saw herself now. Clearly, for the first time in a long time.

And with that vision came the knowledge that she was capable of more—more love, more happiness, more freedom than she had ever believed possible.

Her husband's lack of love didn't mean she was unlovable. It meant he didn't know how to love. And that was his burden to bear, not hers.

As the train slowly pulled into its next station, Meera felt the pull of the future—of the unknown, the possibility of what lay ahead. She wasn't afraid of it anymore. She wasn't afraid of being alone, of facing herself, of living a life without the chains of her past.

She wasn't running away anymore. She was running toward something.

Toward herself.

Mirror- What it says

The train had grown quiet, the soft murmur of conversations fading as most of the passengers drifted into sleep. But for Aryan and Meera, sleep felt impossible. The gravity of their conversation had left both of them wide awake, their thoughts spiraling in directions they hadn't anticipated.

"Do you ever look in the mirror and wonder who you're really seeing?" Aryan asked quietly, his gaze fixed on the darkened window beside him, where his own reflection stared back, ghostly and distant.

Meera's eyes softened with quite grief; her expression thoughtful. "Every day," she replied softly. "But the answer changes, doesn't it?"

Aryan nodded slowly. It did change. The person he saw in the mirror now was not the same person he had been a few years ago. Life had a way of altering the reflection, making it harder to recognize yourself after you'd been through enough.

"Sometimes," Meera continued, her voice barely above a whisper, "when I look in the mirror, I don't even recognize the person looking back at me. It's like… I see the outline, but not the person. Like I'm missing something. Like a part of me has disappeared."

Aryan turned to look at her, sensing the depth behind her words. He understood that feeling all too well—the sense that life had chipped away at you, leaving behind someone you didn't fully recognize.

"Is it the mirror showing us that?" Aryan asked, in a low voice, barely audible to her. "Or is it just reflecting what we feel inside?"

Meera sighed, leaning back in her seat, her eyes distant. "Maybe it's both," she said softly. "The mirror doesn't just show us what's on the surface. It shows us the layers underneath—the things we're carrying, the thoughts we haven't let go of the emotions we try to hide. It's like a movie of your life, playing out right in front of you, whether you're ready to face it or not."

Aryan's heart compressed. He had never thought of it that way, but Meera was right. The mirror was more than just a reflection of his face. It was a reflection of everything he had been through—every memory, every mistake, every fear. It was all there, staring back at him, whether he acknowledged it or not.

"I don't know who I am anymore," Aryan admitted, his voice strained. "Sometimes, when I look in the mirror, I see someone who's lost. Someone who doesn't know what they're supposed to be doing with their life."

Meera nodded, her gaze softening. "We've all felt that way at some point. It's easy to get lost, especially when the things that once defined you no longer make sense. But maybe… maybe it's not about finding who you are. Perhaps it's about accepting the person you've become, even if that person isn't who you thought you'd be."

Aryan looked at her, his chest heavy with emotion. "How do you accept it, though? How do you look in the mirror and make peace with what you see when all you can think about are the things you've lost, the mistakes you've made?"

Meera's eyes filled with understanding. "You stop fighting it. You stop trying to be the person you were before everything fell apart. The mirror isn't lying to you. It's showing you who you are now—the good, the bad, the broken pieces. And it's up to you to decide what to do with that reflection."

Aryan's mind raced. How many times had he looked in the mirror, only to turn away in frustration, in disappointment? He had been clinging to an image of himself that no longer existed. He had been holding onto the past, trying to rebuild what had been broken, instead of accepting the person he had become through the pain, the struggles, and the failures.

"What if you don't like what you see?" Aryan asked, his voice thick with vulnerability. "What if all you see are the mistakes, the things you can't change?"

Meera's lips pressed into a thin line, and for a moment, she didn't answer. Her silence was heavy, filled with the strain of her own experiences, her own regrets. But when she finally spoke, her voice was steady, full of quiet strength.

"You don't have to like everything you see," she said softly. "But you have to face it. The mirror is just a reflection—it shows you the parts of yourself you need to confront. And until you do, you'll keep seeing the same image, the same mistakes, over and over again."

Aryan's felt constricted. Could it really be that simple? Just facing himself, accepting what he saw, and choosing to move forward? It sounded so easy, but the truth was, he wasn't sure he knew how to do that. He wasn't sure he had the strength to look at his reflection and accept the person staring back at him.

Meera's voice broke through his thoughts. "The mirror doesn't define you, Aryan. It doesn't dictate who you are or who you can be. It's just a reflection—a snapshot of a moment in time. But it's not the whole picture. You can change the way you see yourself. You can choose to rewrite the story you've been telling yourself."

Aryan's mind raced. Could he really do that? Could he change the way he saw himself, let go of the past and embrace the future with open arms?

"I guess I'm just scared," Aryan admitted, his voice barely audible. "Scared that I'll never be able to see myself any differently. That no matter what I do, the person I see in the mirror will always be a reminder of the things I've lost."

Meera's gaze softened. "We all have things we've lost, Aryan. We all carry the burden of the past. But you can't let that burden define you. The mirror shows you the scars, yes, but it also shows you the strength it took to survive. You're more than the mistakes you've made. You're the person who lived through them, who's still standing despite everything."

Aryan's heart pounded in his chest. He had spent so long feeling like a failure, like the reflection in the mirror was proof of all the ways he had fallen short. But now, listening to Meera, he wondered if maybe—just maybe—there was another way to see it.

Maybe the reflection wasn't just about the things he had lost. Maybe it was about the things he had gained—the resilience, the wisdom, the strength to keep going even when everything felt like it was falling apart.

"You're right," Aryan said finally, his voice thick with emotion. "I've been seeing the mirror all wrong. I've been looking at it like it's a judgment, like it's showing me everything I've failed at. But it's not. It's showing me that I'm still here. That I'm still fighting. And maybe... that's enough."

Meera smiled; her eyes warm with understanding. "It is enough," she said softly. "And the moment you start believing that the reflection will change. Not because the mirror changes, but because you do."

The quiet settled around them like a soft blanket, but neither Aryan nor Meera seemed ready to let the silence linger for long. The train's gentle motion offered them a kind of sanctuary, a safe space to delve into the questions they had avoided for too long. The night outside the window was pitch black, but here, in the dim light of the train, everything felt exposed.

"I think the hardest part," Meera said slowly, "is seeing yourself for who you really are, not for who others want you to be."

Aryan turned to look at her, sensing the shift in her tone. Her words felt a ton, heavy with meaning, as if she was speaking not just from her own experiences, but from a place of deep reflection.

"Isn't that the hardest part of life?" Aryan asked. "Living as who we truly are, without the masks, without the expectations weighing us down?"

Meera smiled faintly, though it didn't reach her eyes. "Yes," she said softly. "But the world doesn't make it easy, does it? We spend our whole lives trying to fit into roles we didn't choose. We play the part, wear the mask, because it's easier to be what someone else wants than to stand alone."

Aryan's heart ached. He had lived that reality for so long molding himself into what others expected, never asking if it aligned with who he was. He had been shaped by the expectations of his family, his relatives, and even the woman he had tried to love. But none of it had felt right. None of it had felt like him.

"If who I am is what I have, and what I have is lost, then who am I " Aryan said in low tune.

"Who are you when no one's watching?" Aryan asked quietly. "Who is the real Meera, when the mask comes off?"

Meera's expression darkened slightly, a flicker of something vulnerable passing through her eyes. She didn't answer right away, and Aryan could tell that she was searching for the right words, or perhaps the right way to express a truth she hadn't spoken aloud before.

"I don't know," she admitted finally, her voice barely above a whisper. "I've spent so long trying to be what others wanted, I'm not sure who I am anymore. When I look in the mirror, I see… fragments. Pieces of a woman who once knew what she wanted, but who got lost somewhere along the way."

Aryan's chest felt heavy. He could see the pain in her eyes, the encumbrance of the years she had spent trying to meet someone else's expectations. It was a pain he knew all too well.

"I think we all lose ourselves at some point," Aryan said softly. "Life has a way of wearing us down, piece by piece, until all we have left are the fragments of who we used to be."

Meera nodded; her gaze distant as she stared out at the passing darkness. "It's like looking at a broken mirror," she murmured. "You can see pieces of yourself, but none of them fit together. The reflection is fractured, and no matter how hard you try, you can't put it back together the way it was."

Aryan felt a lump form in his throat. That broken mirror—that's what he saw every time he looked at himself. Fractured pieces of a life that no longer made sense, a reflection of someone who had been pulled apart under the pressure of his own failures, his own mistakes.

But sitting here with Meera, he realized something. Maybe the mirror wasn't supposed to be whole. Maybe it wasn't about putting the pieces back together.

"What if we don't need to fix the mirror?" Aryan asked softly. "What if the fragments are enough? What if the broken pieces are just as important as the whole?"

Meera turned to him, her expression softening. "You think the broken pieces matter?" she asked, her voice laced with both curiosity and hesitation.

"I think they do," Aryan said, feeling the words form slowly, thoughtfully. "We spend so much time trying to fix ourselves, trying to erase the things that have hurt us, that we forget that the broken pieces are part of who we are. They tell a story. They show us what we've survived."

Meera's eyes shimmered, and Aryan could see the emotions flickering behind them—emotions she had tried so hard to hide, but that now threatened to surface.

"I've been trying to fix the mirror for so long," she admitted, her voice trembling slightly. "I thought if I could just put everything back the way it was, I would feel whole again. But maybe… maybe you're right. Maybe the fragments are enough. Maybe I don't need to be the person I was before. Maybe I can be something else."

Aryan's chest felt heavy again, but this time it wasn't with sadness. It was with a glimmer of something he hadn't felt in a long time—hope.

"You don't need to be the person you were," Aryan said softly, his voice steady. "None of us do. The past is just a part of the story. It doesn't define who we are, or who we're going to be."

Meera smiled, a small but genuine smile that lit up her face in a way Aryan hadn't seen before. "I want to believe that" she said quietly. "I want to believe that the future can be different, that I don't have to carry the burden of the past with me forever."

"You don't," Aryan said, his heart aching with the truth of his words. "The past only holds us down if we let it. If we keep trying to fix what's already broken, we miss out on the chance to build something new."

Meera's eyes glistened, and for a moment, Aryan wondered if she would cry. But she didn't. Instead, she nodded, her face softening into an expression of quiet acceptance.

"You're right," she said softly. "It's time to stop trying to fix the broken pieces. It's time to start building something new."

And as the train moved steadily into the night, Aryan felt the same sense of acceptance settle over him. The broken pieces didn't need to be fixed. They were part of him, part of his story. And for the first time, he was ready to stop fighting them. He was ready to accept the reflection in the mirror—fractures and all.

The train continued its steady journey through the darkness, the landscape outside still shrouded in the deep black of night. But inside the quiet space they shared, it felt as though the dawn was starting to break. Something had shifted between them—an unspoken understanding, a bond forged through shared vulnerability.

"It's strange," Aryan said quietly, his voice almost lost in the soft hum of the train. "I've spent so many years hating the man I see in the mirror. I've judged him, criticized him, blamed him for everything that went wrong in my life. But now... I don't know. Maybe I've been looking at him the wrong way."

Meera's gaze softened, and she tilted her head slightly as she watched him, her expression thoughtful. "How do you see him now?"

Aryan sighed, running a hand through his hair as he tried to put the feeling into words. "I'm not sure. I think I've been too focused on what I've lost. I kept seeing the mistakes, the failures, the things that didn't turn out the way I wanted them to. But I haven't been seeing the whole picture. I haven't been seeing... the man who survived all of it."

Meera's eyes glinted with something warm, something close to admiration. "That's the thing about the mirror," she said softly. "It only shows us what we choose to see. We get so focused on the flaws, the things we think we should change, that we miss the strength it took to get through the hard times."

Aryan nodded, feeling the truth of her words settle into him. He had been seeing only fragments of himself—the pieces that had been broken, the moments that had shattered his sense of who he was. But those fragments were part of him, part of his story. And they didn't make him weak. They made him whole in a way he hadn't understood before.

"Maybe I've been too afraid to accept that," Aryan said after a pause. "Maybe I've been scared to look at myself and see the things I can't change. But you're right. The mirror only shows us what we're willing to face. And I think I'm ready to face it now."

Meera's heart swelled with empathy as she listened to Aryan. She had been there too lost in the judgment of her own reflection, unable to see the resilience beneath the scars. But now, as she watched him come to terms with his own truth, she felt a sense of hope rise within her.

"I think we both are," she said softly, her voice steady. "We've spent so long running from the past, trying to fix things that aren't ours to fix. But maybe it's time to stop looking for answers in the wrong places. Maybe the mirror isn't where the answers are. Maybe it's just a reminder that we're still here, still fighting."

Aryan looked at her, his expression softening as her words sank in. "Still fighting," he echoed. "That's the part I've been missing. I've been so focused on the losses that I forgot to acknowledge that I'm still here. I'm still fighting, still trying to figure it out."

Meera nodded; her smile gentle but full of understanding. "We all are," she said. "No one has it all figured out. We're all just doing the best we can with what we've been given. And sometimes, the best we can do is accept that the reflection in the mirror isn't perfect. But that doesn't mean it's not enough."

A wave of peace washed over Aryan, and for the first time in decades, he felt the weight on his chest lighten. He had spent years chasing an ideal version of himself, one that didn't exist—one that could never exist. But now, sitting here with Meera, he understood that the man he saw in the mirror wasn't a failure. He was a survivor. And that was enough.

"Do you think the mirror will ever show us the truth?" Aryan asked, his voice thoughtful. "Or will it always be filtered by what we choose to see?"

Meera leaned back in her seat, her eyes drifting toward the window as she considered the question. "I think the mirror shows us a version of the truth," she said slowly. "But it's not the whole truth. It's just a reflection—a moment in time. We're the ones who give it meaning. We're the ones who decide what that reflection says about us."

Aryan felt a warmth spread through him as her words sank in. "So, it's not about fixing the reflection. It's about accepting it. Choosing to see it for what it is, without letting it define us."

Meera nodded, her eyes locking with his. "Exactly. The reflection doesn't define you. You define You. The mirror is just there to remind you of what you've been through, of the person you've become because of it. But it's up to you to decide what that means."

Aryan stared at the window; his reflection barely visible in the dim light. For the first time in years, he didn't turn away. He didn't flinch.

"I think I'm ready," he said softly. "To stop trying to fix the past. To stop chasing the person I used to be."

Meera's heart swelled with a mixture of pride and understanding. She knew how hard it was to face that truth, to let go of the past and embrace the unknown. But she also knew that Aryan was stronger than he gave himself credit for.

"So am I," she whispered, almost to herself. "I'm ready too."

The train rumbled softly beneath them, a comforting rhythm that seemed to echo the steady beat of their hearts. As the night stretched on, the silence between them grew warm, full of unspoken truths and shared understanding. They had both spent so long searching for answers in the wrong places—in the past, in the reflection of a broken mirror. But now, sitting here together, they realized that the answers weren't in the mirror at all. The answers were within them.

And for the first time, that felt like enough.

Who is on the other side

The night outside the train remained impenetrable, a void of blackness that stretched endlessly, mirroring the unknown that both Aryan and Meera felt inside themselves. They had spent hours talking about their pasts, their mistakes, their scars—but now, as the conversation turned inward, they began to confront a question they had long avoided: Who am I, really?

"It's strange," Aryan began, his voice quiet but filled with labored pressure of a thousand unspoken thoughts. "I've lived my whole life trying to be someone. Trying to meet expectations—my own, my family's, society's. But the truth is, I don't even know who I am."

Meera turned her gaze toward him, her expression soft, but her eyes filled with an intensity that matched his own. "I think most of us don't know who we really are," she said softly. "We spend a lot of time trying to become what others expect us to be that we lose sight of ourselves in the process."

Aryan nodded, feeling the truth of her words resonate deep inside him. "Do you ever wonder who's on the other side?"

Meera tilted her head slightly, her brow furrowing in curiosity. "The other side of what?"

Aryan's gaze drifted out the window, staring at his faint reflection in the glass, almost blending with the night. "The other side of fear. Of doubt. Of everything we've been told we should be." He paused, his voice lowering to a near whisper. "Who is on the other side of me?"

Meera exhaled slowly, her breath fogging the window momentarily before it cleared. "Fear," she murmured. "It keeps us in place, doesn't it? It stops us from moving forward, from reaching out for the things we really want. We convince ourselves that we're safe in our comfort zones, but all it does is keep us trapped."

"Fear is everything," Aryan replied, his voice tinged with frustration. "It's been there since I was a child. It was in my parents' voices, telling me to study hard, get a good job, be successful. It was in my decisions—every time I made a safe choice instead of taking a risk, it was fear whispering in my ear, telling me that the world would punish me for stepping outside the lines."

Meera's heart clenched. She could relate. How many times had she stayed silent because she was afraid? How many dreams had she put aside because she feared failure, feared judgment, feared rejection?

"You know," Meera said thoughtfully, "I think fear can be a companion too."

Aryan frowned slightly, his eyes meeting hers. "How, do you mean?"

Meera hesitated for a moment, choosing her words carefully. "I used to think fear was the enemy," she admitted. "But now I'm starting to realize that fear is a teacher. It shows you where your limits are, but it also shows you what's on the other side of those limits. It's not about getting rid of fear—it's about learning to move through it. Fear can tell you what you care about, what you're willing to fight for."

Aryan stared at her, captivated by the quiet strength in her voice. There was a mystery in her words, something that spoke not just of fear, but of possibility. Who was she—this woman who had been through so much, and yet spoke of fear as though it were a guide rather than a barrier?

"I think we spend too much time trying to avoid fear," Aryan said slowly, his voice thoughtful. "We're always running away from it, trying to stay safe. But what if... what if everything we want, everything we've been searching for, is on the other side of it?"

Meera's lips curved into a soft, sad smile, her eyes drifting back to the window. "Maybe that's why we're afraid," she said. "Because deep down, we know that crossing that line—moving past fear—means confronting the truth of who we are. And that's terrifying, isn't it?"

Aryan's heart pounded in his chest. She was right. Moving beyond fear meant facing himself, without the masks, without the expectations. It meant looking at the man he truly was, not the one he had spent his whole life trying to be.

But who was on the other side of him? A better version of himself? Or someone unrecognizable, someone who didn't fit into the neat boxes society had tried to place him in?

"Do you think we can ever truly know who we are?" Aryan asked softly, his voice barely audible over the soft rumble of the train.

Meera didn't answer right away. She closed her eyes for a moment, as if searching for the right words, the right truth to offer him. "I think we can," she said finally, her voice steady but tinged with emotion. "But it's a process. It's not something you just figure out one day and then that's it. It's a journey, a constant unfolding. And maybe that's what makes it so terrifying—because we're never really finished discovering who we are.

There's always another side." Aryan's breath caught in his throat. Her words echoed in the quiet space between them, wrapping around him like a warm, gentle breeze. There was something beautiful in that idea—that self-discovery wasn't a destination, but a journey. A continuous unfolding of layers, each revealing something new, something deeper.

"But what if I don't like who I find?" Aryan asked quietly, his voice betraying the vulnerability he had kept hidden for so long. "What if the man on the other side of fear isn't someone I want to be?"

Meera turned toward him; her expression soft but intense. "Then you keep moving," she said firmly. "You keep searching. You keep peeling back the layers, until you find the part of yourself that you can love. Because that's the only way to truly know who you are—to love yourself enough to face every part of you, even the parts that scare you."

A silence fell between them, but it wasn't the heavy, uncomfortable silence of before. It was a silence filled with possibility, with the unspoken understanding that they were both on the same journey—a journey to discover who they were, not just to each other, but to themselves.

And as the train rumbled on through the night, Aryan couldn't help but wonder—was Meera on the other side of his fear? Was she the mirror he had been avoiding for so long? Or was she something else entirely—something he hadn't even begun to understand?

For now, he didn't need the answer. It was enough to know that the journey had begun.

The train swayed gently, a comforting rhythm that seemed to mirror the ebb and flow of their conversation. Outside, the darkness was thick and impenetrable, but inside, the space between Aryan and Meera felt charged filled with an energy that neither of them fully understood.

"Maybe we never really see ourselves clearly," Aryan said after a long silence, his voice contemplative. "Maybe the person we think we are just a reflection of everything we've been taught to believe. Who we are, who we should be—it's all shaped by the people around us, by society, by our fears. But that's not really us, is it?"

Meera's gaze lingered on him; her eyes soft but intense. "No, it's not," she said softly. "We wear so many masks, don't we? Masks to hide the parts of ourselves we're afraid to show. Masks to protect ourselves from judgment, from disappointment. But the real question is—what's behind the mask? Who is on the other side?"

Aryan felt a shiver run down his spine. It wasn't just a rhetorical question. It was a challenge, a call to action. Who was he, really? Beyond the expectations, beyond the mistakes, beyond the fear? And why did the idea of finding out terrify him so much?

"Do you ever wonder," Aryan began, his voice low, "if the person we're meant to be is someone we've never met? Someone we've been avoiding, hiding from, because we're afraid of what that person might demand from us?"

Meera's heart skipped a beat, the depth of Aryan's question sinking into her like a stone dropping into still water, sending ripples through her thoughts. "I do," she admitted, her voice barely above a whisper. "I wonder all the time. Sometimes I feel like there's a part of me—this other version of me—waiting on the other side of the fear. She's everything I want to be, everything I'm afraid to become."

Aryan's face tensed. He had felt that way too—that sense of potential, of something greater than himself, just out of reach. But it was always accompanied by a sense of dread, a feeling that stepping into that unknown would require him to give up the safety of the life he knew, even if that life no longer fit.

"What if we never find them?" Aryan asked quietly, his voice tinged with vulnerability. "What if we spend our whole lives searching for that version of ourselves and never quite get there?"

Meera's lips curved into a sad smile, her eyes flickering with something close to empathy. "Maybe the point isn't to find them," she said softly. "Maybe the point is to keep searching. To keep moving forward, even when it's hard, even when we don't know who we'll find on the other side."

The air between them grew heavier, as if the conversation had taken on a life of its own, pulling them both into a deeper place—one that neither of them had been prepared for, but that felt inevitable.

"You know," Aryan said, his voice quieter now, "I used to think that the person I was meant to be was someone I could control. Someone I could shape with my choices, my decisions. But now I'm starting to realize that maybe I don't have as much control as I thought. Maybe the person I'm becoming is shaped just as much by the things I can't control—the things that happen to me, the people I meet."

He paused, his eyes drifting toward Meera. "Like you."

Meera's breath caught in her throat, a soft gasp that she tried to hide but couldn't. There it was—the moment she had been waiting for but hadn't expected to come so soon. The quiet acknowledgment that something had shifted between them—that their meeting on this train wasn't just a coincidence, but something deeper, something that neither of them fully understood yet.

"Me?" Meera whispered, her voice trembling slightly.

Aryan nodded, his eyes never leaving hers. "Yeah. You've changed the way I see things. The way I see myself. I don't know if it's because we're both searching for the same things, or if it's because we've been through similar struggles, but... I feel like your part of the journey now. Part of the person I'm becoming."

Meera's heart raced. She had felt the connection too, from the moment they had started talking, but she hadn't expected Aryan to say it out loud, to put words to the quiet understanding that had been growing between them. It made her feel exposed, vulnerable in a way she hadn't been prepared for.

But it also made her feel seen.

"I think we're all shaped by the people we meet," Meera said softly, her voice steadier now. "We carry pieces of them with us, even if we don't realize it. Sometimes those pieces make us better. Sometimes they make us question everything. But either way, they change us."

Aryan's eyes softened, and for a moment, neither of them spoke. The silence between them felt charged, filled with the unspoken questions, the emotions they hadn't yet put into words.

"I'm not sure who's on the other side of me," Aryan said after a long pause. "But I'm starting to think... maybe I'm not supposed to find him alone."

Meera's breath hitched, her heart pounding in her chest. Was he talking about them? About the connection that had been growing between them. Or was it just the philosophical musings of someone searching for meaning in a world that didn't always make sense?

Either way, it made her heart ache—with hope, with fear, with the uncertainty of what lay ahead.

"Maybe none of us are supposed to," Meera replied softly, her voice trembling with the gravity of her own unspoken feelings. "Maybe that's the point. We can't figure out who we are, who we're becoming, without someone else there to reflect it back to us. Someone who sees us... even when we can't see ourselves."

Aryan's pulse quickened, his eyes searching hers as if trying to find the answer to a question he hadn't yet asked. Was she that person? The one who could reflect back the truth of who he was, without judgment, without expectation? Or was she just another fleeting connection, another moment that would pass, leaving him with more questions than answers?

For now, he didn't know. But the mystery of it all—the mystery of her—made him want to keep searching.

The quiet between them deepened, but it wasn't the kind of silence that felt uncomfortable. It was heavy with meaning, with things neither of them could quite put into words but both felt. The train rumbled softly, its motion steady as the night stretched on, but inside, Aryan and Meera were lost in a different kind of journey—a journey toward understanding not only themselves but each other.

"Do you ever wonder," Aryan began slowly, "if the people we meet are mirrors? Not just reflections of ourselves, but reflections of the parts we've been avoiding. The parts we're afraid to face?"

Meera's heart skipped a beat, her gaze locking with his. "Mirrors," she echoed softly. "That's an interesting way to put it."

Aryan nodded; his brow furrowed as he tried to articulate the thought that had been circling his mind. "I think sometimes we see in other people the things we can't see in ourselves," he said, his voice thoughtful. "The parts we're trying to run from, the parts we don't want to admit are there. But maybe that's why we need those people—to reflect back the truth of who we are, even when we're not ready to see it."

Meera's breath caught in her throat. His words hit her in a place she hadn't expected—deep inside, where her own fears and insecurities had been buried for so long. Was Aryan her mirror? Was that why she had felt so drawn to him from the moment they had met? Because he reflected the parts of her that she had been afraid to confront—the parts that wanted more, that needed more?

"Maybe that's why it's so hard," Meera said quietly. "Because sometimes the reflection isn't what we want to see."

Aryan's eyes softened, a flicker of understanding passing between them. "Yeah," he murmured. "Sometimes it's easier to turn away from the mirror than to face what it's showing us."

Meera's heart ached. She had spent years turning away from her own reflection—not just the physical reflection, but the reflection of who she truly was. She had tried so hard to be the person her husband wanted, the person society expected her to be, that she had lost sight of herself in the process.

But now, sitting here with Aryan, she felt like she was beginning to see herself again—not the version she had been trying to fix, but the version that had been hidden beneath all the layers of expectation and fear.

"Who do you see when you look at me?" Meera asked softly, her voice trembling with vulnerability. "What am I reflecting back to you?"

Aryan's breath hitched, his eyes searching hers. It was a question he hadn't been prepared for, but it was a question he had been asking himself since they had met. What was it about Meera that made him feel so exposed, so seen?

"I see someone who's stronger than she knows," Aryan said quietly, his voice filled with emotion. "I see someone who's been through hell and come out the other side. But I also see someone who's afraid—

afraid of wanting more, afraid of what it would mean to let go of the past."

Meera's eyes filled with tears, though she quickly blinked them away.

He saw her.

He saw the parts of her that she had tried so hard to hide, the parts that still ached with the scars of her past. But he also saw her strength, her resilience—the things she had forgotten about herself.

"And what about you?" Meera asked softly, her voice steady despite the emotion coursing through her. "What do you see when you look in the mirror?"

Aryan's breath felt strained, his throat suddenly dry. He had spent so long avoiding that question, so long turning away from the reflection that showed him everything he didn't want to face. But now, with Meera sitting across from him, her eyes filled with an understanding that made him feel safe, he couldn't hide anymore.

"I see someone who's been running for a long time," Aryan admitted, his voice thick with emotion. "Someone who's been afraid to stop and face himself because he's not sure if he'll like what he finds. I see the mistakes, the regrets, the things I wish I could change. But... I also see hope. I see someone who's still trying. Someone who hasn't given up."

Meera's heart swelled with empathy. She had seen that in him from the beginning—the quiet determination, the struggle to keep going even when everything felt broken. He was stronger than he gave himself credit for, just as she had been stronger than she realized.

"Do you think we'll ever stop running?" Meera asked softly, her eyes filled with a mixture of hope and uncertainty.

Aryan smiled faintly, though there was a sadness in his eyes. "I don't know," he said quietly. "But I think maybe… we don't have to run alone."

Meera's breath caught in her throat at his words, a subtle but undeniable shift in the air between them. There it was—that quiet, unspoken connection that had been growing since they had met. It wasn't just about shared experiences, or the way they reflected each other's fears and hopes. It was something more. Something deeper.

"Maybe we don't," Meera whispered, her voice trembling slightly with shouldered load of what she was feeling. "Maybe that's why we found each other. Not to fix each other, but to remind each other that we're not alone."

Aryan's eyes softened, his heart pounding in his chest. He hadn't expected this. He hadn't expected to find someone who saw him so clearly, someone who reflected not just his flaws, but his potential—someone who made him feel like he wasn't alone in the journey anymore.

"Maybe that's the other side," Aryan said softly, his voice filled with wonder. "Not the version of ourselves we've been chasing, but the connection we've been missing. The reminder that we don't have to figure it all out by ourselves."

Meera's heart raced, her mind swirling with a mixture of emotions—hope, fear, anticipation. Was this the other side? The place where they stopped running, stopped hiding, and simply allowed themselves to be seen—by each other, by themselves?

For the first time ever, she wasn't afraid of the answer.

They didn't need to know all the answers yet. It was enough to know that they weren't alone in the search.

The train continued its gentle sway, but something had changed between Aryan and Meera. The silence that settled over them now felt different, filled with a quiet understanding, a shared recognition of the journey they were both on—a journey that no longer felt so lonely.

"It's strange, isn't it?" Aryan said softly, his voice breaking through the quiet. "How can two strangers see each other so clearly?"

Meera smiled, her eyes softening. "Maybe we're not strangers after all," she replied. "Maybe we've just been waiting to find the mirror that shows us who we really are."

Aryan's heart pounding against his chest, the impact of her words settling over him like a blanket of truth. She was right. They had been searching for themselves in all the wrong places, looking for answers in the past, in their mistakes, in the versions of themselves they had tried to fix. But maybe the answers had always been in each other—in the quiet reflection of their shared fears and hopes.

"Maybe," Aryan murmured, his voice barely audible over the soft hum of the train. "Maybe we're finally ready to see who we really are."

As the train rumbled forward into the unknown, Aryan and Meera sat together in silence, their hearts full but their minds calm. They didn't need to figure everything out tonight. For now, it was enough to know they had found someone who understood them, someone who could see past the masks and the fears to the truth beneath.

They weren't on the other side of fear yet. But they were closer than they had ever been.

As the night moved into maturity, the soft golden lights of the cabin casting a warm glow over Aryan and Meera. But with the light came the sharp return of reality—the expectations, the roles they had been trying to live up to for so long.

Expectations had always defined them—who they were supposed to be, how they were supposed to act. From their families, from society, from themselves. But now, after the quiet revelations of the night, both Aryan and Meera felt an unspoken tension of those expectations pressing down on them in a new way.

"Do you ever feel like you're living someone else's life?" Aryan asked suddenly, his voice cutting through the stillness of the morning.

Meera turned to him, her expression thoughtful. "All the time," she replied quietly. "But it's easier to live up to other people's expectations than to face your own."

Aryan nodded, understanding all too well. The expectations they had been running from—the ones they had spent their whole lives trying to meet—were starting to feel heavier.

But now it seems, it was time to stop carrying them.

The Expectations

The lights from the streets filtered softly through the train windows, casting soft shadows across the seats. The silence between Aryan and Meera was no longer heavy, but thoughtful. After the night of intense conversations, they had both begun to peel back layers of themselves they hadn't realized were there—layers shaped by expectations they had spent their whole lives trying to meet.

"I've been wondering about expectations," Aryan said suddenly, breaking the stillness. His voice was low, reflective, as if he were speaking more to himself than to her. "How much of our lives are defined by them, and how often they set us up to fail."

Meera turned to him, her brow furrowing slightly. "What do you mean?"

Aryan sighed, running a hand through his hair as he gathered his thoughts. "I think… by setting expectations, we often set ourselves up for disappointment. We imagine how things should be, how people should act, and then, when they don't live up to that image, we're left feeling let down. It's like we create a version of reality in our heads, and when the real world doesn't match up, it all falls apart."

Meera nodded slowly, perceiving the gravity of his words. "You're right," she said quietly. "Expectations can kill relationships before they even start. We fill our heads with all these ideas of what we want and how we want things to be, but life... life doesn't work that way."

She paused, staring out the window at the passing scenery, her thoughts drifting to her own failed marriage. How many times had she set expectations for her husband, only to be disappointed when he didn't meet them? How many times had she imagined a version of love that didn't align with the reality of their relationship?

"Life doesn't make sense," she murmured, almost to herself. "It never does. You take what it gives you, and sometimes that could be someone completely unexpected. Someone who turns your world upside down for the better."

Aryan felt his breath strained. He knew exactly what she meant. "But when we expect things from people," he said slowly, "we lose the ability to truly see them. We see the version of them we've created in our heads, not the person they really are."

Meera nodded, her eyes filling with a sadness that Aryan recognized all too well. "And when they don't meet those expectations," she continued, "we start to resent them for it, even though they never asked us to place those expectations on them in the first place."

Aryan's mind raced back to his own past, to the times he had built up expectations for how things should be, for who his parents should be. He had wanted them to fit into the image he had created—perfect, supportive, never flawed—and when they inevitably couldn't, he had felt betrayed. But it wasn't them that had failed him—it was the illusion of perfection he had been chasing.

"I think expectations are tied to ego," Meera said, her voice heavy with realization. "We want things to be a certain way, not because it's what's best, but because it's what our ego tells us we deserve. And when reality doesn't match up, the ego gets angry. It tells us we've been wronged."

Aryan's gaze gleamed with recognition. "It's true. We want people to fit into our world, to fulfill the role we've imagined for them, instead of letting them just... be. It's the ego that singles someone out and makes them special, using them as a way to avoid our own pain, our own insecurities."

Meera felt a knot tighten in her chest. That was exactly what she had done. She had used her husband as a way to cover up the emptiness inside her, the feeling of not being enough. She had placed expectations on him to fill the void, to give her what she couldn't give herself—self-worth, validation, love (or whatever it is called).

"But when he couldn't give me that," Meera said, her voice thick with emotion, "I blamed him. I thought he was the one making me unhappy, but really, it was me. It was the pain inside me that I didn't want to face."

Aryan's heart ached for her, because he understood. He had done the same thing with his parents—expected them to fix the parts of himself that were broken, to fill the emptiness that had nothing to do with them.

"The ego uses people as a shield," Aryan said softly. "It uses them to cover up the constant underlying feeling of discontent, of not being enough. But at some point, it stops working. The illusion breaks, and suddenly, everything falls apart."

Aryan's mind drifted back to his past, the one that had left him shattered. He had thought he was doing more than expected, thought they were everything he needed. But when the initial excitement faded, the discontent came rushing back, stronger than before. And instead of facing it, he had projected his unhappiness onto them. He had convinced himself that they were the problem, that they weren't doing enough, weren't living up to his expectations.

"But the problem wasn't them," Aryan said, his voice barely a whisper. "It was me. I was using them to cover up my own pain, my own fear of not being enough. And when they couldn't meet the expectations, I had set for them, everything fell apart."

Meera's eyes filled with tears, though she blinked them away. "We all do that".

Aryan noticed her eye filling up, he added, "You know, we use love to avoid surrender. We use it to avoid facing the parts of ourselves that we don't want to acknowledge. But true love—the kind of love that goes beyond ego—that's the kind of love that doesn't ask for anything in return. It's not about wanting or needing. It's about seeing someone for who they are, without expecting them to change."

Meera felt a lump form in her throat. Could such a love exist? A love without expectation, without the need to possess or control? A love that allowed the other person to be exactly who they were, flaws and all?

"That kind of love sounds… impossible," Meera said softly, her voice filled with doubt.

Aryan smiled sadly; his eyes filled with a wisdom that came from years of heartache. "It's not impossible," he said quietly. "But it's rare. Because it requires us to surrender—to let go of our ego, our need to control, our fear of not being enough. It requires us to face ourselves, fully and completely, and accept that we are whole, even without someone else completing us."

Meera's mind raced, trying to wrap itself around the idea of love without expectation, without ego. Was she capable of that? Was anyone?

"I've never experienced that kind of love," Meera admitted, her voice filled with vulnerability. "All only relationship has been based on wanting, on needing. On trying to fill the emptiness inside me."

Meera's gaze softened, and for a moment, she didn't speak. She simply looked at him, as if trying to see past the layers of pain, past the expectations he had carried for so long.

"Maybe we don't choose who we love," Aryan said softly, his voice trembling with emotion. "Maybe it just happens. Maybe the purest kind of love isn't something we plan or expect. It's something that finds us, when we're ready to let go of everything we've been holding onto."

Meera felt a grip around her chest. She wanted to believe her, wanted to believe that love could be something more than what she had never experienced, more than the cycle of expectation and disappointment she had been trapped in for so long.

"But how do we let go?" Meera asked, her voice thick with emotion. "How do we let go from being controlled, from the fear of not being enough?"

Aryan smiled gently; his eyes filled with warmth. "We stop," he said simply. "We stop fighting. We stop trying to be available and we let life happen. We accept that we are whole, as we are, and that love—true love—will come when we stop looking for it. When we stop expecting it to fill the emptiness inside us."

Meera's breath caught in her throat, and for a moment, she didn't know what to say. Could it really be that simple? Could letting go of expectations, letting go of the need to be available, really lead to something deeper, something more fulfilling?

Aryan's words echoed in her mind: "We don't choose who we love. It just happens."

Maybe that was the answer. Maybe love wasn't something to be chased or forced. Maybe it was something that found you, when you were ready to surrender—when you were ready to let go of the expectations that had been holding you back.

The soft glow of the lights felt almost intrusive as it spilled across the train compartment. Aryan watched it with quiet detachment, feeling the sharp contrast between the peacefulness of the night and the turbulence inside him. His mind wouldn't quiet down. Not after everything he had said to Meera. Not after the realization that he had spent his entire life building a fortress of expectations—only to find himself trapped within it.

"Expectations," he whispered to himself, the word tasting bitter in his mouth. He thought back to all the moments in his life that had been shaped by expectations—his family's, his friends', his own. They had been like invisible chains, pulling him in directions he hadn't chosen but had followed anyway, because that's what was expected.

His parents had expected him to continue fulfilling their expectations; to follow the well-disguised path they had laid out for him. Study hard, get a good job, marry a good woman—the classic formula for a life that looked perfect on the outside, but felt hollow on the inside. And for the most part, Aryan had complied. He had met every expectation—on the surface. But deep down, something had always been missing. A sense of fulfillment, of being truly seen for who he was, not for the roles he played.

He glanced at Meera, who sat across from him, her eyes half-closed as she leaned back against her seat. She looked peaceful, but Aryan knew from their conversations that peace had been hard-won for her.

He could still hear her voice in his head, soft but filled with conviction:

"Expectations can kill relationships before they even start."

Those words had struck him like a blow to the chest. How many relationships had he killed before they had the chance to bloom? How many times had he entered into one with a checklist, with a set of expectations that no one could ever meet? And when those expectations weren't fulfilled, how quickly had he withdrawn, convincing himself that the other person wasn't right for him?

He had thought he was protecting himself, setting standards, making sure he wouldn't get hurt. But in reality, he had been building walls—walls that kept people out, walls that kept him safe, but also isolated.

"It's the ego, isn't it?" he murmured, thinking back to what Meera had said. "The ego sets the expectations."

Meera's words echoed in his mind, words that had shaken something loose inside him. "The ego singles someone out and makes them special. It uses them to cover up the constant feeling of discontent, of not being enough."

He exhaled deeply, the realization settling over him like a cold wave. That's exactly what he had done in every relationship. He had singled someone out, made them "special" in his mind, placed them on a pedestal and expected them to meet all of his unspoken needs. He had made them responsible for his happiness, for filling the emptiness inside him. And when they couldn't—when they inevitably failed—he had turned away, convinced that they weren't the one.

It was never about them, though. It was about him. About his fear of not being enough. About his ego, trying to use someone else to cover up the pain he had been carrying all along.

"I was so wrong," Aryan muttered under his breath, he felt a sharp pain as the memories of past relationships flooded back. The subtle fights. The growing discontent. The way love had turned into frustration and, eventually, resentment.

He had always believed that the other person was to blame. That they were the ones who weren't trying hard enough, who weren't loving him the way he needed to be loved. But now, sitting here with Meera's words echoing in his mind, he realized it had never been about them. It was him.

His expectations—his ego—had poisoned every relationship he had been in. He hadn't been searching for love. He had been searching for validation. For someone to tell him he was enough, that he mattered, that he was worthy of being loved. And when his partners couldn't give him that trust, when they couldn't fill the void inside him, he had convinced himself they were the problem.

But it wasn't them. It was always him.

"Expectations," Aryan repeated, this time louder, almost as if he were testing the word, trying to see how it felt in the light of this new understanding.

He thought back to his last relationship—the one that had ended so badly. He had walked into it with his heart full of hope, convinced that this time, it would be different. He had found someone who seemed to fit every requirement, someone who checked all the boxes on his mental list of what a perfect partner should be. She was beautiful, kind. But overtime, the cracks began to show.

She wasn't as attentive as he had hoped. She didn't always say the right things. She had her own life, her own struggles, and sometimes, she wasn't there for him in the way he needed. And instead of accepting her for who she was—for the imperfect, flawed, but beautiful person she was—Aryan had started to withdraw. He had let his expectations color his perception of her, and when she didn't meet them, he had blamed her.

"It wasn't fair," he whispered, his voice thick with guilt. "It wasn't fair to her."

Meera stirred beside him, her eyes fluttering open as she glanced over at him. "What wasn't fair?" she asked softly, her voice still thick with sleep.

Aryan hesitated for a moment, unsure if he was ready to voice the thoughts swirling in his head. But something about Meera—the way she listened without judgment—made him feel safe, made him feel like he could speak his truth without fear of being misunderstood.

"My expectations," he admitted, his voice barely above a whisper. "In all my relationships. I... I set these impossible expectations, and when they weren't met, I blamed the other person. I thought they weren't enough. But really, it was me. I wasn't enough—not for them, not for myself."

Meera's gaze softened, and she nodded slowly, her expression filled with understanding. "We all do that," she said gently. "We expect people to fill the gaps inside us, to make us feel whole. But no one can do that. No one can fill those gaps for you."

Aryan nodded, feeling his heart compressed as he processed her words. He had been trying to fill those gaps his whole life—first through success, then through relationships. But no matter how much he achieved, no matter how much love he thought he had found, the emptiness always remained.

"I've been running from myself," Aryan said, his voice trembling with the unspoken depth of the admission. "I thought if I could just find the right person, the right job, the right… anything… that it would fix me. That it would fill the emptiness. But it never did."

Meera's eyes softened even more; her gaze filled with empathy. "Because it can't," she said softly. "No one else can make you feel whole. That has to come from within."

Aryan's chest ached with the truth of her words. He had been searching for something outside himself, something that didn't exist. And in the process, he had lost sight of who he was.

"I don't even know who I am anymore," Aryan admitted, his voice thick with emotion. "I've spent so long trying to be what everyone else wanted me to be, trying to meet expectations—my own, my family's, society's—that I don't even know who I am without them."

Meera smiled gently; her eyes filled with warmth. "That's because you've been looking in the wrong place," she said softly. "You've been searching for yourself in other people, in their expectations of you. But the truth is, who you are isn't defined by anyone else. It's something only you can find."

Aryan's heart clenched. He had been looking for himself in all the wrong places—in love, in success, in the approval of others. But now, he realized that the answers he had been searching for weren't outside him. They were inside, waiting for him to stop running, to stop hiding behind the expectations that had controlled his life for so long.

"How do I find him?" Aryan asked softly, his voice filled with vulnerability. "The man I'm supposed to be?"

Meera's smile was soft, but her eyes were steady. "You let go of the expectations," she said simply. "You let go of the need to be anything other than who you are, right now, in this moment. You stop trying to be enough for everyone else, and you start being enough for yourself."

Aryan's breath caught in his throat, and for a moment, he didn't know what to say. Could it really be that simple? Could letting go of expectations—letting go of the need to be perfect, to be loved, to be validated by others—really be the key to finding himself?

As he sat there, the train rumbling softly beneath him, Aryan realized that maybe it wasn't about finding the right person, or the right life. Maybe it was about finding the courage to let go. To let go of the expectations that had been holding him back, and to finally allow himself to be free.

The train's rhythmic hum continued, a steady backdrop to the storm of thoughts swirling in Aryan's mind. He sat quietly, staring out the window as the moon light painted the landscape in soft hues of blues and black. The conversation with Meera had left him raw, exposed—but not in a way that frightened him. Instead, it felt like a peeling back of layers he hadn't realized were there, layers he had hidden behind for so long.

"Letting go," Aryan repeated to himself, the words both a comfort and a challenge. It was strange to think that the very thing he had been holding on to— the expectations, the need to be enough—was the thing keeping him from truly understanding himself. Could he really do it? Could he let go of the need to prove something to the world, to others, to himself?

For eon, his worth had been tied to those expectations. But now, sitting here, with the quiet strength of Meera beside him, he felt something shift. It wasn't a dramatic, life-changing epiphany. It was subtle, like the soft glow of the morning light, gentle but undeniable. He could let go. He didn't have to be defined by anyone else's standards, not even his own.

It wasn't about being enough for others anymore. It was about being enough for himself.

"It's not easy, is it?" Meera's voice broke through the silence, soft and understanding.

Aryan turned to her; his heart heavy but lighter than it had been in a long time. "No, it's not," he admitted.

"But I think it's the only way forward. I've spent so long trying to meet everyone else's expectations that I've forgotten what it feels like to just... be. To just exist without the pressure of proving something."

Meera nodded; her eyes warm with empathy. "It's a process. Letting go doesn't happen overnight. But once you start, once you allow yourself to release those expectations, everything starts to change. You start to see the world, and yourself, differently."

Aryan smiled faintly, feeling the truth of her words settle into him. "I think I'm ready for that," he said quietly. "I'm ready to see things differently."

As the train rolled forward into the new day, Aryan and Meera sat in a comfortable silence, both lost in their thoughts. There was still so much to figure out, so much to understand. But for the first time, Aryan felt like he was on the right path. He didn't need all the answers right now. All he needed was the willingness to let go of the expectations that had been weighing him down for so long.

And with that thought, Aryan felt something new stir inside him—a question that had been building throughout the night, but that he hadn't yet allowed himself to ask. It was a question about love, about what it really meant, about what it could be without the burden of expectations and ego.

As he glanced at Meera, who was gazing out the window, lost in her own thoughts, he knew that love—true love—was more than he had ever understood it to be.

The Deliberation on Love

The soft glow of moonlight filtered through the windows, bathing the train compartment in a blue hue that seemed to mirror the warmth of their conversation. Aryan sat in thoughtful silence, his mind turning over the words Meera had said, trying to make sense of everything they had discussed. The concept of love—true love, ego, and expectations—was no longer as simple as it once had seemed.

"I found out recently," Aryan began softly, breaking the quiet between them, "that there are two kinds of love."

Meera turned to him, her eyes curious, but not surprised. "Two kinds?" she echoed, prompting him to continue.

"Yes," Aryan nodded, feeling the truth of it settle into him. "There's the kind of love most people know, the kind that's all-consuming and passionate. Romantic love. But it's tied to ego, to expectations. That's the love we all chase, isn't it? The one that makes you feel alive, but also burns you out. The one that's based on needing something from the other person."

Meera's expression softened, and Aryan could tell she knew exactly what he meant. "Romantic love is the kind of love most people think they need," she said quietly. "But it's also the kind that leads to disappointment, because it's tied to wanting, to desire. And when those desires aren't met, the love turns into something else—frustration, resentment, even hate."

Aryan nodded, the weight of his experiences pressed down on his chest, heavy and unrelenting. "That's what happened to me," he admitted, his voice thick with emotion. "In what I had experienced, I thought love was about wanting, about someone fulfilling me, making me feel whole. But the more I wanted, the more disappointed I became. It wasn't fair."

Meera's eyes softened with understanding. "Romantic love," she murmured, "is tied to ego. It's based on wanting something from the other person—whether it's validation, security, or just the feeling of being wanted. But that kind of love can't last, because it's always dependent on the other person giving you something. And when they don't, it falls apart."

Aryan leaned forward; his hands clasped tightly in his lap. "Exactly," he said, his voice trembling slightly. "But then I started to wonder… what if there's another kind of love? A kind that doesn't depend on wanting or needing. A love that's pure, that's about connection at a deeper level, beyond the ego. The kind of love where you don't have expectations, where you don't need anything from the other person, but you still feel complete."

Meera smiled softly; her eyes filled with a quiet wisdom. "That kind of love does exist," she said, her voice steady. "It's rare, but it's real. I call it pure love—the kind that goes beyond ego, beyond wants and demands. It's not about what the other person can give you, but about seeing them, truly seeing them, and loving them for who they are, not for what they can do for you."

Aryan's chest felt heavy, a sudden wave of emotion washing over him. Could he really believe that such a love existed? Could he find it? "Pure love," he repeated, the words feeling foreign but comforting on his tongue. "I've never experienced that. I've always thought love had to be about wanting, about being consumed by the other person. But maybe… that's where I've been wrong."

Meera's eyes softened, and she leaned back slightly, her gaze drifting out the window. "Most people never find pure love," she said quietly. "They spend their lives chasing romantic love, thinking that it will complete them. But that kind of love is based on ego, on expectations. It's fragile, because it depends on the other person fulfilling your needs. And when they don't, the illusion breaks."

Aryan exhaled slowly, he felt the gravity of her words settle over him. "I've been living in that illusion," he admitted, his voice barely above a whisper. "I've been looking for someone to complete me, to make me feel whole. But I never realized that the love I was searching for couldn't come from outside me. It had to come from within."

Meera nodded; her gaze filled with compassion. "That's the difference between romantic love and pure love," she said softly. "Romantic love is about filling a void, about trying to escape the emptiness inside. But pure love—true love—is about seeing the other person, not as someone who can fill your emptiness, but as someone you can share your wholeness with. It's about connection, not possession."

Aryan felt a lump form in his throat, the truth of her words hitting him harder than he had expected. He had spent his whole life searching for love in all the wrong places, thinking that it had to come from someone else, that it had to be about wanting and needing. But now, sitting here with Meera, he realized that love wasn't about filling a void. It was about connection, about being present with the other person without trying to make them into something they weren't.

"I've been looking for the wrong kind of love," Aryan said quietly, his voice thick with emotion. "I've been looking for someone to give me what I couldn't give myself. But that's not love, is it? That's ego. That's wanting someone to fix me, to make me feel whole. But love... love isn't about that. Love is about accepting the other person as they are, without needing them to change, without wanting them to fulfill some part of you that's missing."

Meera smiled gently; her eyes filled with warmth. "That's exactly it," she said softly. "Love, real love, isn't about wanting or needing. It's about surrender. It's about letting go of the ego, the desire to control or to be controlled, and just being with the other person. It's about seeing them for who they are, and loving them, completely and unconditionally."

Aryans hear swelled with warmth, a wave of clarity washing over him. "I've never done that," he admitted, his voice trembling. "I've never loved someone without wanting something from them. I've never just... surrendered."

Meera's eyes softened, and she reached out, gently placing her hand on his. "It's not easy," she said quietly. "Letting go of the ego, letting go of expectations... it takes time. But once you do, something changes. Something shifts inside you, and you start to see love differently. It's no longer about what you can get from the other person. It's about what you can give. As I said, It's about connection, not possession."

Aryan swallowed hard, his mind racing. Could he, do it? Could he let go of everything he had been holding on to, everything he had believed about love? Could he let go of his need to control or to be controlled, to expect, to want?

"I don't know if I can," he whispered, his voice barely audible.

Meera smiled; her gaze filled with understanding. "It's not something that happens overnight," she said softly. "But the fact that you're willing to try... that's the first step. Love isn't about perfection. It's about the journey. And the journey begins with surrender."

As the train continued its journey through the moon light, Aryan and Meera sat in silence, their hands resting gently together. For the first time, Aryan felt a sense of peace settle over him—a peace that came from understanding, from letting go. He didn't have all the answers yet. But he was starting to see love differently. It wasn't about ego. It wasn't about expectations.

It was about surrender.

And perhaps, that was enough.

Aryan stared out the window, his gaze following the rolling hills and trees as they passed by, but his thoughts were far from the peaceful landscape.

Inside, his mind was a storm of emotions—an unexpected, uninvited conflict that had been quietly building ever since he met Meera. There was something between them, something unspoken but undeniably real. He felt it in the way she looked at him, in the pauses between their words, in the quiet moments where their silence said more than their conversations ever could.

But love? Could this really be love?

No, it couldn't be. He shook his head slightly, almost as if he could shake away the idea itself. Love didn't happen like this—so suddenly, so quietly. Love was supposed to be a whirlwind, a rush of emotions that swept you off your feet, left you breathless. What he was feeling now was something else entirely—something slower, deeper, more unsettling.

Yet, the more he tried to push it away, the more he couldn't deny that it was there, growing between them like a quiet flame that neither of them was willing to acknowledge. It wasn't the kind of love he had known before. It wasn't driven by passion or lust or the desperate need to possess someone. This was different calmer, yet somehow more intense. It was in the way he felt at ease around Meera, the way her presence soothed something deep inside him that he hadn't even realized was unsettled.

And that scared him more than anything.

"This can't be love," Aryan thought, his mind racing. "Not after everything I've been through." He had spent years searching for love, only to end up disappointed and heartbroken. How could something that felt so calm and peaceful be love? Wasn't love supposed to be complicated, messy, full of highs and lows?

But as he glanced at Meera, who sat quietly beside him, lost in her own thoughts, he couldn't shake the feeling that what he was experiencing was, in fact, something deeper than anything he had known before. There was a connection between them, one that went beyond words, beyond the surface-level attraction he had felt in past relationships. This was different. It wasn't about wanting or needing her—it was about simply being with her.

And that too was terrifying.

"Love shouldn't feel this easy," Aryan thought, his chest grew heavy as the realization sank in. "It shouldn't feel like surrender." But wasn't that exactly what Meera had been talking about? That love wasn't about possession or control, but about letting go, about allowing the other person to be exactly who they were without expecting anything in return?

He had never experienced love like that before. His past experience had always been about filling a void, about finding someone to make him feel whole, to validate his worth. But this... this was different. With

Meera, he didn't feel the need to prove anything. He didn't feel the pressure to be perfect, to meet some unspoken expectation. He could just be himself—flawed, broken, and still trying to figure out who he was. And somehow, that was enough.

But could it really be love? Aryan's mind rebelled against the idea, as if admitting it would somehow make it less real. He didn't want to fall in love again, not after everything he had been through. Love had always brought pain, disappointment, and the crushing realization that the person he had placed all his hopes in wasn't capable of fulfilling them. He had learned the hard way that love, or at least the kind of love he had known, was fleeting. It couldn't be trusted.

But this feeling with Meera was nothing like the love he had known before. It wasn't driven by need. He didn't want anything from her—at least, nothing that came from a place of emptiness or longing. He just wanted to be near her, to share this quiet space with her, to know that she saw him for who he was, and didn't turn away.

And she didn't turn away. That was the most unsettling part of it all. She saw him—truly saw him—and she stayed.

Aryan's heart felt an emotional rush as he looked at Meera, who was now watching the scenery pass by outside the window. There was a softness in her, a quiet strength that drew him in, even though he didn't fully understand why. It wasn't just her beauty—although he couldn't deny that there was something captivating about the way her hair fell softly over her face, or the way her eyes seemed to hold entire worlds within them. It was something deeper than that—something he couldn't quite put into words.

"This can't be happening," he thought again, more desperately this time. "I'm not ready for this." But even as the thought crossed his mind, he knew it wasn't true. He wasn't afraid of love. He was afraid of the kind of love that Meera represented—a love without conditions, without expectations, without the need for control.

That kind of love required vulnerability. It required him to let go of everything he had been holding on to—his fears, his insecurities, his need to protect himself from getting hurt again. And that was terrifying.

"You're thinking too much again." Meera's voice broke through his thoughts, soft and gentle, but with a knowing edge.

Aryan blinked, startled by the sudden interruption, and turned to face her. "What?"

Meera smiled, though there was a hint of sadness in her eyes. "You've been quiet for a while," she said softly. "You've got that look again—the one you get when you're trying to figure something out, but you don't want to admit what you've already discovered."

Aryan's heart skipped a beat, her words cutting through him like a blade. She knew. Somehow, without him even saying a word, she knew what was going on inside him. She always did. That was part of what scared him so much—the way she seemed to understand him, the way she could see through all the walls he had built up over the years.

"I'm just... thinking," Aryan muttered, though he knew it was a weak response.

Meera's smile didn't falter, but her eyes softened even more. "You're thinking about us, aren't you?"

A flush of surprise rushed through Aryan, and for a moment, he didn't know how to respond. Us. The word felt heavy, filled with possibility, with hope, but also with fear. Was there an "us"? Or was it just something he had imagined, something he had projected onto their connection because it was easier to explain than the quiet, inexplicable feeling growing between them?

"I don't know what's happening," Aryan admitted, his voice low, almost a whisper. "I don't know how to explain it."

Meera turned toward him, her expression unreadable, but her eyes were filled with something deep, something real. "You don't have to explain it," she said softly. "Sometimes, things just are. We don't always need to put a name to them."

Aryan's body tensed. Could he accept that? Could he let go of the need to define what was happening between them, to categorize it as love or something else? Could he just let it be?

But the fear lingered—the fear of surrender, of giving in to something he didn't fully understand. He had spent so long trying to protect himself from being hurt again, from falling into the trap of loving someone only to have them leave, or to have love fade into something unrecognizable. How could he trust this? How could he trust himself?

"I've been here before," Aryan thought, his mind flashing back to all the times he had believed he was in love, only to watch it crumble before his eyes. The idea of love had always seemed so clear, so certain—until it wasn't. But this felt different. This wasn't the consuming passion he had known before. It wasn't driven by the need to be loved, to be wanted. It was quieter, more subtle. And somehow, that made it even more terrifying.

"Do you think this is love?" Aryan asked suddenly, the words escaping his lips before he could stop them.

Meera blinked, surprised by the directness of the question, but she didn't look away. "I don't know," she said after a long pause. "Maybe. Maybe not. Does it matter?"

Aryan's heart pounded in his chest. Did it matter? He had always thought that love needed a name, that it needed to be defined in order to be real. But maybe Meera was right. Maybe this feeling between them didn't need to be called anything. Maybe it just was.

"I guess not," Aryan murmured, though his voice lacked conviction. Aryan's words hung in the air, as if he were waiting for Meera to say something that would pull him out of his own thoughts, something that would make sense of what he was feeling. But she didn't speak. Instead, she simply looked at him with that same quiet understanding, the one that made him feel like she saw every part of him—the parts he hadn't been ready to face.

"I guess it doesn't matter," Aryan repeated, though his heart wasn't sure he believed it. How could it not matter? Love had always mattered to him—it had shaped his choices, defined his happiness, and broken him more times than he cared to admit. And now, as he sat here with Meera, the feeling was growing again, in a way that terrified him.

Because this time, it felt real.

But Aryan couldn't shake the memories of his past—the relationships that had started with passion and hope, only to unravel into disappointment and resentment. How many times had he believed he was in love, only to find himself wondering where it had gone, where it had all gone wrong?

"Love fades," Aryan thought, his chest aching. "It always does." No matter how strong the connection felt in the beginning, no matter how deeply he believed in it, love had a way of slipping through his fingers, leaving behind nothing but the hollow ache of what could have been.

"But this is different, isn't it?" The question echoed in his mind, and he hated how much he wanted the answer to be yes. He wanted to believe that this—whatever this was with Meera—could be different. That it didn't have to follow the same pattern, the same cycle of expectation, disappointment, and loss.

But he had been here before. Hadn't he?

"You're afraid," Meera said softly, her voice gentle but firm, as if she could hear his thoughts as clearly as if he had spoken them aloud.

Aryan's heart skipped a beat. How did she know? How could she always see through him like this?

"Afraid of what?" he asked, though he knew the answer.

"Afraid of letting go," Meera replied, her gaze steady. "Afraid of what will happen if you surrender. You're afraid of love, Aryan. And it's okay."

Aryan's breath caught in his throat, and for a moment, he couldn't speak. She was right. He was afraid. Terrified, actually. Not of love itself, but of what it required of him—vulnerability, surrender, the willingness to let go of control.

He had spent most of his life trying to protect himself from the pain that love inevitably brought. Every time he had let himself fall, he had ended up broken, wondering if it was worth it. And now, with Meera, he could feel himself on the edge of that same precipice, teetering between the safety of his walls and the terrifying freedom of letting them fall.

"What if it's not enough?" Aryan whispered, his voice trembled, burdened by the enormity of the question . "What if I'm not enough?"

Meera's gaze softened, and she reached out, gently taking his hand in hers. The warmth of her touch sent a shiver through him, grounding him in the moment, pulling him back from the spiral of doubt and fear that had gripped his mind.

"You are enough," she said simply, her voice filled with quiet conviction. "You don't have to be perfect. You don't have to have all the answers. Love isn't about being enough, Aryan. It's about being present.

It's about showing up, even when you're scared, even when you don't know what's going to happen."

Aryan's chest brimmed with emotions, a lump forming in his throat. He wanted to believe her—he wanted to believe that love could be as simple as that, as pure as just being there for someone, without the need to be perfect or to meet some impossible standard. But the scars of his past were hard to ignore.

"But what if it's not real?" Aryan asked, his voice barely above a whisper. "What if I'm just imagining this? What if it's all in my head?"

Meera smiled gently; her eyes filled with understanding. "It's real," she said softly. "But you're not ready to see it yet. And that's okay."

Aryan's breath caught, the raw honesty in her words cutting through him. She wasn't pushing him, wasn't demanding anything from him. She was giving him space to feel what he needed to feel, to process the conflict inside him at his own pace.

And somehow, that made it even harder to deny what was happening between them.

"This isn't how love is supposed to feel," Aryan thought, his mind rebelling against the quiet certainty that was settling into his heart. "Love is supposed to be chaotic, passionate, overwhelmingly loud. It's supposed to consume you."

But this—this connection he felt with Meera—wasn't chaotic. It wasn't overwhelming in the way he had always thought love should be. It was quieter, more subtle. It was a slow burn, a feeling that crept up on him when he wasn't looking, a connection that made him feel more grounded, more himself.

And that scared him.

Because if this was love, if this was what real, pure love felt like, then everything he had believed about love before was wrong. And if he had been wrong about love, what else had he been wrong about?

"I don't know if I'm ready for this," Aryan admitted, his voice barely audible. "I don't know if I'm ready to feel this way again."

Meera didn't pull away, her hand still resting gently on his. "You don't have to be ready," she said softly. "Love isn't something you plan for. It's not something you prepare for. It just happens. And when it does, it doesn't ask if you're ready."

Aryan swallowed hard; his heart ached as her words sank in. She was right. He wasn't ready. He didn't know if he would ever be ready. But that didn't change the fact that something was happening between them—something he couldn't ignore, no matter how hard he tried.

"But what if I'm not enough?" Aryan whispered again, the fear that had been gnawing at him spilling out before he could stop it.

Meera's eyes softened, and she squeezed his hand gently. "You are enough," she said firmly, her voice steady. "You've always been enough. You just have to believe it."

Aryan's heart clenched, the vulnerability in her words cutting through him. He had spent his whole life chasing love, chasing validation, chasing the feeling of being enough for everyone else. But now, sitting here with Meera, he realized that love wasn't something to be chased. It wasn't something to be earned or proven.

Love was something to be felt—quietly, deeply, without expectations, without demands.

"Maybe that's what this is," Aryan thought, his mind finally starting to accept the truth that had been staring him in the face all along. "Maybe this is love."

But it wasn't the kind of love he had known before. It wasn't driven by passion or desire or the need to possess someone. It was softer, more patient. It was a connection that didn't demand anything from him, that didn't ask him to be anything other than who he was.

And for the first time in his life, Aryan felt like that was enough.

The train rumbled softly beneath them, the steady rhythm lulling them into a peaceful silence. Aryan and Meera sat together, their hands still intertwined, neither of them needing to speak.

The connection between them was undeniable, even if they weren't ready to fully name it. It was there, in the quiet moments, in the spaces between their words, in the way they saw each other without judgment or expectation.

Love was happening, even if they both weren't ready to admit it. And maybe, Aryan thought, that was okay. Maybe love didn't need to be defined. Maybe it didn't need to be understood or explained.

Maybe love just was.

The silence between them stretched out, comfortable and unspoken, as the train continued its gentle journey. Aryan could feel the significance of everything that had been said, and yet there was a sense of lightness too, as though acknowledging his fears had somehow made them easier to bear. The tension he had been holding onto for so long began to ease. He didn't have to define what was happening between him and Meera. He didn't have to label it or understand it fully.

Love was happening, that much he knew. But it wasn't the kind of love he had chased before—the kind that demanded answers, clarity, and certainty. This love was different, quieter, but more powerful for it. It didn't ask anything of him. It didn't need him to be perfect or whole. It simply allowed him to be.

Meera shifted beside him, her gaze still fixed on the world passing by outside the window, but Aryan could sense the quiet peace she radiated. She wasn't rushing him. She wasn't trying to force him into anything. She was just there, beside him, present in a way that made him feel safe.

He glanced down at their intertwined hands, the simple connection grounding him in the moment. For so long, he had believed that love had to be all-consuming, overwhelming—something that swept you off your feet and left you breathless. But now, he was beginning to understand that love didn't have to be loud to be real. It didn't have to burn bright to last.

"I don't need to be afraid," Aryan thought to himself, the realization settling into him like a slow, deep breath. "I don't need to protect myself from this." For the first time in a long time, he felt a sense of calm, as though the constant pressure to define, to control, to expect something from love had finally lifted.

"Maybe this is what love looks like," Aryan mused, his gaze drifting over to Meera. "Maybe love isn't about what you can take, but what you can give. Maybe it's about showing up, not because you want something in return, but because you simply want to be there."

And that's what this felt like with Meera. He just wanted to be there—with her, beside her, sharing the quiet moments without needing anything from her. It was a strange feeling, unfamiliar and unsettling, but it also felt... right.

Meera glanced at him, sensing his eyes on her. Her smile was soft, knowing, as though she understood exactly what was going through his mind without him having to say a word.

"You're over thinking it again," Meera said gently, her voice light but warm. "You don't have to figure it all out."

Aryan smiled, though it was more to himself than to her. "I know," he said quietly. "I'm just... not used to this."

"Not used to what?" Meera asked, her brow furrowing slightly in curiosity.

"Not used to feeling like this," Aryan admitted, his voice low but steady. "Feeling... okay with not knowing. With not needing to have all the answers."

Meera's smile widened slightly, her eyes softening with understanding. "That's the thing about love," she said. "It doesn't need answers. It doesn't need to be figured out. It just is."

Aryan nodded, feeling a quiet peace settle over him. For a long time, he had been searching for clarity, for certainty. But now, he was starting to realize that love—true love—wasn't something you could contain. It was something you simply had to let be.

The train continued its journey, the world outside passing by in a blur of color and light, but Aryan was no longer lost in his thoughts. He was here, fully present in this moment, and for the first time, that was enough.

He didn't need to figure out what was happening between him and Meera. He didn't need to name it or control it. Whatever it was—whether it was love or something else—he was willing to let it unfold in its own time, without the pressure of expectations or the fear of what might come next.

"Thank you," Aryan said softly, turning to Meera with a quiet smile.

Meera raised an eyebrow, her eyes filled with curiosity. "For what?"

"For being here," Aryan replied, his voice filled with sincerity. "For… everything."

Meera's smile softened, and she squeezed his hand gently. "You don't need to thank me," she said quietly. "I'm exactly where I want to be."

As the train continued to move forward, so did Aryan's heart. He was no longer afraid. He was no longer running from love, from the vulnerability it required. He was ready to surrender, to let go of the expectations that had weighed him down for so long.

And as he sat there, hand in hand with Meera, Aryan knew that whatever happened next—whether this was love or something else—he would be okay. He didn't need to have all the answers.

Sometimes, love was just about being there. About showing up. About letting go.

And for now, that felt enough.

The Stolen Time

The concept of time had always puzzled Aryan, but lately, it had begun to take on a new meaning.

Sitting beside Meera, with the world passing by outside the train window, he couldn't help but think about how much of his life he had spent running out of time, chasing after moments that seemed to slip through his fingers, never fully present in any of them.

He had always been too busy looking forward, planning for the future, or dwelling on the past to appreciate what was right in front of him.

"What is time, really?" Aryan mused aloud, his voice barely above a whisper.

Meera turned to him; her expression thoughtful. "Moments," she said simply. "Moments are created by time, Time is nothing more than a collection of moments, but have you ever wondered what are these moments? Is it from the past, present or the future? I think it is how we experience those moments that makes all the difference."

Moments.

Aryan let the word sink in. "But how many of those moments do we miss?" he asked, his voice tinged with regret. "How many times have I let the present slip away because I was too focused on what came before or what might happen next?"

"Time poverty is a problem partly of perception and partly of distribution". Aryan said in a low tone.

"We live in a time, where we are constantly running around the clock but never seem to find time. Our daily lives are full of time. We are surrounded by time from getting up in the morning until checking the alarm clock in the night."

Aryan continued, "when time is seen as tangible and often given less priority over other things then many grow stingy with the former to maximize the latter. People who tend to give more time to their work, tend to feel more antsy when they are not busy".

Meera's gaze softened, and she nodded in quiet understanding. "We all do that," she said gently. "We struggle to spend time, not the clock time but the real time- Quality time."

She continued, as Aryan noticed her eyes sparkled, " and some live in assumed future, while wanting to be there, they let go of the present moment. "

"We live everywhere except in the present. We're either stuck in the past, replaying old memories, or we're constantly thinking about the future, trying to predict what's coming. And in doing so, we forget to live in the present or rather in the moment. And the future depends on the quality of our present moment."

Aryan frowned, her words hitting him hard. "The quality of the present moment," he repeated, turning the phrase over in his mind.

For so long, he had believed that life was built on grand moments, monumental events that would change everything in an instant.

But now, he was beginning to see that life wasn't about the big moments at all. It was about the small, seemingly insignificant ones—the ones he had been too busy to notice.

The present moment is of quality if we are fully present. Being in the moment is the key to spiritual awakening, or to say the least, to live happier and to live more liberated life -read freedom.

"We waste so much time," Aryan murmured, his voice thick with regret. "Chasing after things that don't matter, while letting the moments that do slip away."

Meera smiled, though there was a hint of sadness in her eyes. "That's the thing about time," she said softly. "We think we have so much of it, but really, it's fleeting."

"The only time we truly have is right now. This moment."

She paused, looking out the window at the passing landscape.

"The present moment is of quality if we are fully present. Being in the moment is the key to spiritual awakening, or to say the least, to live happier and to live more liberated life - freedom."

Meera continued, her fingers tracing her bracelet, "Many don't realize that we waste millions of quality moments for an assumed future or for unchangeable past. These very moments that they are neglecting are what actually creates the future but not that many know this."

Aryan's felt a lump in his throat as he listened to her words. How many small moments had he missed? How many times had he been so focused on achieving something, on becoming someone, that he had forgotten to appreciate what was right in front of him? The present moment—the one thing he had always taken for granted.

"It's like we're always stealing time," Aryan said suddenly, his voice growing more thoughtful. "We steal time from the present to invest it in the future, but the future never arrives the way we imagine it. And by the time we realize it, all those stolen moments are gone."

Meera nodded slowly; her expression thoughtful. "That's true," she said. "But there are also those who understand the value of time."

" They are like time robbers, every day they go through the grind, but discreetly, all day long, stealing little bits of time throughout the day—quiet moments of reflection, brief moments of joy—so when night falls, they go to their corners, where no one can see them, they takeout the "loot", count each moments of time they had stolen and cherish them."

Aryan leaned back in his seat, her words sparking something inside him. "It's like selling stolen time in darkness of night to buy some precious moments. As if they are trying to auction their "loot" to would be bidders, bidding on the quality. So, it's not about time itself," he said slowly.

"It's about how we spend it. How present we are in those moments."

Meera's eyes sparkled as she looked at him, a soft smile playing on her lips.

"Aren't we all too busy chasing the ultimate happiness – wonder what that is – but while doing so, we all miss seeing the millions of small moments of happiness. Whereas it is right there, in front of us but we fail to see – we are all short sighted."

"You know," Meera continued, with profound depth in her eyes, "These little moments in life aren't really little. They are the cornerstone of our days and they create the life we live. They gradually paint the masterpiece - called life.

And yet we mistakenly believe that only the big things make a profound difference."

Aryan listened with deep sense of understanding, he reflected that he needs to open his eyes and relish what he sees. Enjoy the little things that are happening around him, because its not how much we have, rather how much we enjoy that makes the difference.

Aryan leaned forward, his voice thoughtful, "Its like celebrating the small victories and cherishing the seemingly insignificant moments, for you'll one day realize that these were the big moments. Appreciate the small things because they add up to everything. No moment is "mundane", or ordinary, each has its own curiosity, interest and awe."

Meera smiled, a warmth spreading through her chest, "Exactly," she said. "Small things matter—small acts of kindness, moments of compassion, selfless giving, half-steps in the right direction—and when we do them mindfully, purposefully, and with love, we can make a big difference."

Meera's continued, looking ever so gracious, "You don't have to do something momentous or monumental to change the world. You can begin one step at a time to transform the smallest areas of your life, or the life of someone else.

As the saying goes, "Friendship isn't a big thing. It's a million little things."

Aryan resonated her words and said, " its funny how we often wait for something big, something sensational to happen to make that change- change that we only think about but never want. But that's not true, as you said, it's the little things, small, insignificant things that matters a lot."

Meera, a quite joy settled on her face, said, "These small "anything" moments are to be collected and treasured, Aryan.

As life happens moments by moments, each day is one small step. Value these moments and grow on them. A good life is a collection of happy moments and being available in those moments."

The word hit Aryan with surprising force—available. How often had he been physically present in a moment, but mentally or emotionally somewhere else? How many times had he missed out on truly connecting with the people in his life because he wasn't available, because he was too busy thinking about something else?

As the train continued its journey, they both fell into a comfortable silence, the conversation's impact slowly sank in, leaving a lingering tension. It was as though they had found a way to reclaim something precious - not by chasing time, but by simply being there for it.

Aryan felt a quiet sense of gratitude wash over him. He felt like he was truly living in the moment.

He wasn't running out of time. He wasn't missing out on life. He was here, fully available, in this moment.

They weren't thinking about tomorrow or dwelling on yesterday, they were there, together, fully present, and for the first time in a long while, time felt like it was on their side—and that seemed enough.

The Availability

As the train moved steadily onward, Aryan found himself lost in thoughts, reflecting on the conversations he and Meera had shared throughout the journey. They had discussed relationships, love, time, and the weight of expectations—but now, as the morning seems marching toward the world outside, another question crept into his mind.

"Availability," he murmured to himself, the weight of the word sinking in. "Why is it a must that someone must be always available to have a relationship? Why is that its mostly expected of one to be available for the other? If that is the case then, is the relationship true?

Meera tilted her head slightly, her expression curious. "What do you mean?"

"I mean..." Aryan hesitated, searching for the right words, "I've always been so focused on doing things, achieving things. I've never really thought about just... being. About being available in each moment, fully present, without thinking about what's next."

Meera smiled softly, her eyes filled with understanding. "That's the key," she said gently. "It's not about doing more. It's about being more. Being more present, being more available—to the people in your life, to the moments that matter."

Aryan felt a lump form in his throat, the truth of her words hitting him hard. "I've missed so much," he whispered, his voice thick with emotion. "I've been so focused on the next thing, the next goal, that I haven't really been here. I haven't been available—not to myself, not to the people who matter."

Meera's gaze softened, and she reached out, gently placing her hand on his. "It's never too late to start," she said quietly. "The beautiful thing about the present moment is that it's always here, waiting for you. All you have to do is show up."

Aryan exhaled slowly, her words filling him with a sense of quiet peace. For so long, he had been chasing time, trying to control it, trying to make the most of it. But now, he was beginning to understand that time wasn't something to be controlled or chased. It was something to be embraced, something to be lived in.

And that meant being available. Fully available—to the moments, to the people, to the life that was happening around him, right here and now.

The train continued its steady journey, the world outside passing by in a blur of green and gold, but Aryan no longer felt like time was slipping away from him. Instead, he felt anchored in the present, more aware of the moment than he had ever been before.

Meera smiled, her gaze steady. "Exactly," she said softly. "Because when you're fully available, you're not just living—you're truly experiencing life. And that's where the magic happens."

What did it mean to truly be available? Was it about showing up physically? Or was there something deeper, something more essential about emotional availability—about being open, vulnerable, and present in a way that transcended the superficial?

Aryan turned these questions over in his mind, the idea of availability suddenly feeling more complex than he had ever considered. "And what happens when the other person isn't available as much as you are or as much as you like?" Aryan thought, "so, what is availability then? Is it being just physically available or being emotionally available actually matter? "What does it mean to be available in a relationship?" he wondered, his chest heavy with the weight of the question.

Meera, sensing his silence, glanced at him with a curious expression. "What's on your mind?" she asked gently.

Aryan hesitated for a moment, still trying to form his thoughts into something coherent. "Availability," he said finally. "What does it really mean? I feel like I've always thought of it in a very narrow way—as just being there, physically. But now, I'm not so sure."

Meera's expression softened, her eyes filling with understanding. "It's much more than that," she said quietly. "Being available physically is the easy part. But being emotionally available—that's the real challenge."

Aryan nodded, the truth of her words sinking in. He had been physically present in most of his relationships—showing up on occasions, conversations, and shared moments. But emotionally? He wasn't so sure. How many times had he been distracted by his own thoughts, his own fears, even while sitting right beside someone he claimed to love? How often had he been too guarded to let the other person see the real him, to be vulnerable in the way that truly mattered?

"I think emotional availability is harder for most people," Aryan said slowly, his voice thoughtful. "It's easy to show up, to be there physically. But letting someone in, really letting them see you… that's terrifying."

Meera smiled gently, her eyes filled with a quiet understanding. "That's because being emotionally available means risking something," she said softly. "It means letting go of control. It means allowing yourself to be seen—not the version of yourself that you present to the world, but the real, flawed, imperfect version. And that's scary. Because once you let someone see the real you, there's a chance they might not like what they find."

Aryan's felt choked, her words hitting him harder than he expected. That was it, wasn't it? The reason he had always kept people at arm's length, the reason he had never fully opened up, even to the people he loved. It was fear. Fear of rejection, fear of not being enough, fear of being seen for who he really was.

"It's easier to stay closed off," Aryan admitted, his voice low. "It's easier to keep a part of yourself hidden, to only show the parts you think are acceptable."

Meera nodded, her gaze steady. "But when you do that," she said gently, "you're never truly available to the other person. You're there physically, but emotionally, you're distant. And that creates a disconnect—a gap that can't be bridged unless both people are willing to be fully present, fully available, in every sense."

Aryan's mind raced, reflecting on his past relationships. How many of them had failed because of that gap, that emotional distance he had been too afraid to cross? He had always thought the problem was with the other person, that they weren't giving him what he needed. But now, he was beginning to see that the problem wasn't them—it was him. He hadn't been available.

"I've been too scared to be available," Aryan said quietly, more to himself than to Meera. "I've been afraid to let people in. And because of that, I've always felt disconnected, like something was missing."

Meera's expression softened, and she reached out, gently pressing her hand on his. "We all have our defenses," she said softly. "We all build walls to protect ourselves from getting hurt. But those walls don't just keep out the pain—they also keep out love, connection, intimacy. The very things we're searching for."

Aryan exhaled slowly reflecting on his past relationships. How many of them had failed because of that gap, that emotional distance he had been too afraid to cross? He had always thought the problem was with the other person, that they weren't giving him what he needed. But now, he was beginning to see that the problem wasn't them—it was him. He hadn't been available.

Aryan exhaled slowly, her words resonating deeply within him. He had built walls around himself for so long, convinced that they were keeping him safe. But now, he was starting to see that those walls had done more harm than good. They had kept him isolated, trapped in his own fear and insecurity, unable to truly connect with anyone.

"So, what do we do?" Aryan asked, his voice thick with emotion. "How do we break down those walls? How do we become truly available?"

Meera smiled, her gaze filled with warmth. "It starts with vulnerability," she said simply. "It starts with being willing to show up, fully and completely, even when it's scary. It means being honest with yourself and with the other person, even when you're afraid of what they might think. It means taking down the walls, brick by brick, and trusting that the other person will meet you there."

Aryan's heart pounded, the vulnerability in her words cutting through him. Could he do that? Could he let go of his defenses, of the fear that had kept him closed off for so long? Could he be available—not just physically, but emotionally?

It wasn't just about being there for someone else, he realized. It was about being there for himself, too. About being present with his own emotions, his own fears, his own desires. He had to be available to himself before he could be available to anyone else.

"But what about the other side of it?" Aryan asked suddenly, his voice more curious now. "What happens when someone isn't available? What do you do when the other person can't or won't show up in the same way?"

Meera's expression shifted, becoming more reflective. "That's the hard part," she admitted. "Because as much as we want to believe that availability is a choice, sometimes it's not. Sometimes people are emotionally unavailable because they're afraid, or because they've been hurt, or because they just don't know how to be any other way. And when that happens, it can feel like you're reaching out into empty space, waiting for something that might never come."

Aryan frowned, the truth of her words sinking in. "So, what do you do?" he asked softly. "How do you handle being in a relationship with someone who isn't available?"

Meera sighed softly, her gaze distant for a moment. "You have to decide if it's worth it," she said quietly. "You have to ask yourself if you're willing to wait, if you're willing to keep showing up, even when the other person can't or won't. But at the same time, you also have to set boundaries. You have to protect your own heart, your own well-being. Because if you keep giving and giving without receiving anything in return, eventually, you'll lose yourself."

Aryan with heavy voice, "Boundaries," he repeated, thinking back to all the times he had sacrificed his own needs for the sake of a relationship. He had always thought that being available meant being selfless, giving everything he had, even when it hurt. But now, he was starting to see that true availability wasn't about self-sacrifice. It was about balance. It was about showing up for someone else while also showing up for yourself.

"You can't pour from an empty cup," Meera said softly, her eyes locking with his. "If you keep giving and giving without taking care of yourself, without setting boundaries, eventually, there's nothing left to give. And that's when resentment starts to build. That's when you start feeling like a victim."

Aryan nodded slowly, her words hitting home. He had been there before—in relationships where he had given everything, only to feel empty and resentful when the other person couldn't or wouldn't give back. But now, he understood that it wasn't their fault. It was his. He hadn't set boundaries. He hadn't protected himself. He had been too available—too willing to sacrifice his own needs for the sake of someone else's.

"So, it's about balance," Aryan said softly, his voice filled with a new sense of understanding. "It's about being available, but also knowing when to step back. It's about showing up for someone else, but also making sure you're taking care of yourself."

Meera smiled, her eyes warm with approval. "Exactly," she said. "Availability isn't about being there all the time, or giving everything you have. It's about being present—physically, emotionally, and mentally—in the moments that matter. But it's also about setting boundaries, knowing your limits, and protecting your own heart."

Aryan exhaled slowly, a sense of peace settling over him. For so long, he had believed that being available meant sacrificing himself, giving everything he had, no matter the cost. But now, he was beginning to see that true availability was about balance—about being present and open, but also knowing when to protect yourself, when to step back, when to say no.

"It's all about balance," Aryan repeated, his voice filled with quiet certainty. "Being available doesn't mean losing yourself. It means showing up, fully and completely, without giving too much."

Meera nodded, her smile soft and knowing. "Exactly," she said. "Because when you're truly available—both to yourself and to others—that's when real connection happens. That's when love becomes possible."

The train continued its journey, the world outside a blur of movement, but inside, Aryan felt a sense of stillness. He was learning, slowly but surely, how to be available—not just for someone else, but for himself. And that, he realized, was the key to everything.

True availability wasn't about always being there. It was about knowing when to show up, and knowing when to step back. It was about balance. And for the first time, Aryan felt like he was ready to find that balance.

The Paradigm of Problem

Meera had been sitting in silence for quite some time now, her gaze distant as the train rolled on, carrying them deeper into the journey. Aryan could sense the heaviness in her, the way her thoughts weighed on her shoulders like an invisible burden. She had been quiet for a while now, her usual spark dimmed, and though she hadn't said anything, Aryan could feel that something was bothering her. She was lost in her own world of pain—a place Aryan had visited many times himself.

"What's on your mind?" Aryan asked gently, breaking the silence between them.

Meera glanced at him, her expression softening, but her eyes still clouded with something she wasn't ready to name. "I don't know," she admitted, her voice low. "I've just been thinking about... everything. My life, my choices, the things I can't seem to fix. It's like I'm always fighting the same battles, over and over. No matter what I do, the problems never go away."

Aryan leaned in, sensing the depth of her frustration. He could see the pain behind her words, the sense of being stuck in a cycle of struggle, unable to break free. He had been there before, feeling like no matter how hard he tried, he couldn't escape his problems. But now, after everything he had been through, he understood something that had taken him years to learn.

"Maybe the problem isn't the problem," Aryan said quietly, his voice thoughtful.

Meera raised an eyebrow, her curiosity piqued. "What do you mean?"

"I mean," Aryan began, choosing his words carefully, "sometimes it's not the problem itself that's the issue. It's the way we look at it. The way we approach it."

Meera frowned, clearly not convinced. "So, what—you're saying my problems aren't real?"

"No, no," Aryan said quickly, shaking his head. "I'm not saying that at all. Your problems are real—believe me, I know they're real. But sometimes the way we perceive a problem makes it bigger than it needs to be. We get so caught up in how overwhelming it feels that we lose sight of the fact that every problem, no matter how big, has a solution."

Meera sighed, her thoughts pressed down on her, overwhelming her with their weight. "It just feels like... no matter what I do, there's always something else. One problem gets solved, and another one pops up. It's exhausting."

Aryan nodded, understanding her frustration. "I get that. I've felt that way too. But what I've learned is that problems are inevitable. We're never going to live a life without them. The trick isn't to avoid problems—it's to change the way we think about them."

Meera looked at him, her eyes narrowing slightly in thought. "Change the way we think about them?" she repeated. "How do you do that?"

Aryan smiled, sensing a small shift in her resistance. "By seeing them as opportunities, instead of roadblocks. When we stop looking at problems as something that's stopping us, and start seeing them as something we can grow through, everything changes."

Meera's expression softened, though there was still doubt in her eyes. "It's not that easy," she said quietly. "Some problems feel impossible to get past. Some things... they just feel too big."

Aryan's heart ached at the vulnerability in her voice. He could feel the depth of her pain, the past had shaped her into someone who bore too much, her burdens visible in her every step, who expected every challenge to be another reason to struggle. But Aryan also knew that the size of the problem wasn't what mattered—it was the size of her perception of it.

"I know it's not easy," Aryan said softly. "But it's possible. You know the old saying—'The way you see the problem is the problem'? It's true. When you see a problem as insurmountable, that's what it becomes. But when you see it as something you can learn from, something that's pushing you toward growth, it stops being something to fear. It becomes a stepping stone, not a roadblock."

Meera's eyes flickered with something—hope, maybe, or curiosity—but the doubt was still there. "But how do you do that?" she asked, her voice tinged with frustration. "How do you change the way you see something that's causing you so much pain?"

Aryan leaned in closer, his voice gentle but firm. "You start by accepting that problems are a part of life," he said. "No one gets through life without them. And the pain they cause—that's real. But instead of letting that pain paralyze you, you can use it to propel you forward. Problems aren't here to stop you, Meera. They're here to teach you something."

Meera's gaze dropped to her hands, and Aryan could see the internal battle she was fighting. She wanted to believe him—wanted to believe that her pain wasn't in vain, that there was something on the other side of all the struggles she had faced. But years of hurt, of feeling stuck, had left her with a hardened layer of doubt.

"What can I possibly learn from all this?" Meera asked quietly, her voice breaking slightly. "All I've learned is how to endure. How to keep going, even when everything feels impossible."

Aryan's chest felt heavy, her pain palpable. He had been in that place before—the place where survival felt like the only option. But he had also learned that survival wasn't the end of the story. Survival was just the beginning.

"Endurance is important," Aryan said gently. "But it's not everything. Surviving is one thing—but thriving, learning, growing—that's where the real power is. Problems can teach us about ourselves, about what we're capable of, if we let them. They can show us strengths we didn't know we had. But we can't see that if we're only focused on the pain they cause."

Meera looked at him, her eyes softening as she listened. "So, you're saying I've been focusing on the wrong thing?"

Aryan smiled, but there was a sadness in it. "I think we all do that, at some point. We get so caught up in the pain of the problem that we miss the lesson it's trying to teach us. But once you shift your focus—even just a little—you start to see that the problem itself isn't the enemy. It's just a tool."

Meera's brow furrowed, as if she were turning his words over in her mind. "A tool for what?"

"A tool for growth," Aryan replied softly. "A tool to help you become the person you're meant to be. Every problem you face has the potential to teach you something—about yourself, about others, about the world. But you have to be open to that. You have to stop seeing problems as something that's happening to you and start seeing them as something that's happening for you."

Meera exhaled slowly; her shoulders sagged slightly as the meaning of his words sank in. "I don't know if I can do that," she admitted, her voice barely above a whisper. "I've spent so long fighting against everything—against every challenge, every setback. It's hard to imagine not feeling like the world is against me."

Aryan's heart ached for her, but he also knew that she was standing on the edge of a breakthrough. "It's not about flipping a switch," he said gently. "It's about taking small steps. It's about changing the way you approach each problem, one at a time. Instead of asking, 'Why is this happening to me?' start asking, 'What is this teaching me?'"

Meera's gaze softened, and for the first time, Aryan saw a glimmer of something else in her eyes—something that looked like hope. "I don't know if I can change overnight," she said softly. "But I think I can try."

Aryan smiled, a warmth spreading through him. "That's all you need to do," he said. "Just try. One problem at a time. One step at a time."

Meera nodded, her gaze drifting back to the window as the train carried them forward. "I'll try," she whispered, more to herself than to him.

And in that moment, Aryan knew that she was already beginning to see things differently.

The problems in her life hadn't disappeared, but her perception of them had started to shift. And that, Aryan realized, was where real change began.

Trust - The Emotional Collapse

Trust. The word seemed to hang in the air between them, carrying with it the weight of unspoken fears, past disappointments, and an undeniable need for something deeper. Aryan sat in silence for a moment, reflecting on what trust really meant. It wasn't something that came easily—not to him, not to Meera. Both of them had been burned by it, had seen trust fracture into a thousand pieces when life didn't go the way they had planned.

But here they were, talking about trust, as if it were something they could rebuild together.

"The thing you said about trust," Meera began softly, her voice filled with a quiet vulnerability, "made me think about how much it impacts everything."

Aryan glanced at her, sensing that this was something she had been mulling over for a while. "It does," he agreed, his voice low but steady. "Trust can make or break a relationship."

Meera nodded, her eyes distant as she looked out the window. "I never thought about it before," she admitted. "Not like this, anyway. I always thought trust was just... there. You either had it or you didn't. But now, I'm realizing it's something you have to nurture. It's not just a given."

Aryan listened carefully, understanding exactly what she meant. Trust had always felt like a fragile thing in his life, something that could be shattered with a single misstep. And once broken, it was almost impossible to put back together the same way. He had learned that the hard way, in relationships where trust had been abused, where promises had been made and then broken.

But there was another layer beneath the surface.

"Have you ever felt like everything inside you is broken?" Aryan asked quietly, his voice suddenly filled with the thickness of something he hadn't spoken aloud in a long time. "Like you've hit rock bottom, emotionally?"

Meera's eyes flickered with recognition, and Aryan knew immediately that she understood. "Why did it happen?" she murmured, more to herself than to him. "Why did I hit rock bottom?"

There was a silence between them, the kind of silence that spoke louder than words. Meera's expression hardened slightly, her gaze drifting downward as she wrestled with something from deep within. "It's strange," she began slowly. "We call it an emotional breakdown, as if it's just a phrase we throw around when we don't know how else to describe the feeling.

But it's real, isn't it? When you reach that point where everything inside feels broken, like you can't convey what's going on. You're just... completely shattered."

Aryan nodded, his heart heavy with memories of his own emotional collapse. "I've been there," he said softly. "I know what it's like to hit that point where you feel totally broken inside. Where it feels like nothing can fix it."

Meera exhaled slowly, her shoulders drooped, weighed down by everything she had carried for so long. "And the hardest part is," she continued, "when you feel like you've lost trust in everything—yourself, the people around you, the world. It's like you're standing on the edge of a cliff, looking down, wondering if anything will ever feel solid again."

Aryan's heart felt tight. He had stood on that cliff many times, his heart pounding with the fear that he wouldn't be able to pull himself back from the edge. Trust—real trust—felt impossible when you were in that place. It was one thing to talk about trust, to understand it intellectually, but when your heart had been shattered, when you had collapsed emotionally, trust became something almost mythical. How could you rebuild trust in a world that had already broken you?

"I think that's what makes trust so fragile," Aryan said after a long pause. "When you've been through something like that—when you've hit rock bottom emotionally—it's hard to believe that trust can exist again. You start to question everything."

Meera nodded, her eyes distant as she lost herself in the memories of her own collapse. "There were times," she whispered, "when I thought I would never be able to trust again. Not in people, not in myself. Everything felt so... shattered. And the worst part was that I didn't even know how to put the pieces back together."

Aryan reached out, his hand covering hers, and for a moment, neither of them spoke. The silence was heavy with shared pain, with the unspoken understanding that they had both been to that place—the place where trust had crumbled.

"So, what do we do?" Meera asked softly, her voice trembling slightly. "How do we rebuild trust when we've been broken like that?"

Aryan thought about it for a moment, his mind racing through the experiences of his past, the moments where trust had been lost and found again. "It starts small," he said finally, his voice quiet but steady. "It starts with the little things. Showing up, being honest, even when it's hard. It's not something you can rebuild overnight. But piece by piece, you can start to put it back together."

Meera looked at him, her eyes filled with a mixture of hope and fear. "But what if it breaks again?" she asked, her voice barely above a whisper.

Aryan squeezed her hand, his expression soft but resolute. "It might," he admitted. "There's always that risk. But trust isn't about guarantees. It's about choosing to believe in the possibility that it can be different this time. It's about being willing to take that risk, even though you know it could hurt."

Meera's eyes filled with tears, and Aryan could see the internal struggle playing out on her face. "I want to trust again," she whispered. "I want to believe that it's possible."

"It is," Aryan said softly, his voice filled with quiet conviction. "But it takes time. And it takes both of us, showing up every day, being honest, being vulnerable. Even when it's hard. Especially when it's hard."

Meera nodded, a single tear slipping down her cheek. "I'll try," she whispered to herself. "I'll try to trust again."

As the train continued its steady journey, Aryan and Meera sat in comfortable silence, their hands intertwined. They didn't need to say anything more—the understanding between them was enough. Trust was something they would build together, piece by piece, moment by moment.

And in that trust, they found the foundation for something real, something lasting.

The War Within

The silence between them stretched out, heavy with unspoken words. The rhythmic clattering of the train on the tracks provided a steady backdrop to the storm swirling inside their minds. Aryan leaned back in his seat; his distant gaze revealed the pressure of his own thoughts pressing down. It was the war within—the constant, agonizing conflict that seemed to split him in two. He knew Meera felt it too. They were both at war with themselves, battling the same inner turmoil, though their reasons were different.

"Do you ever feel like you're fighting yourself?" Aryan asked quietly, his voice barely cutting through the sound of the train.

Meera turned to him, her eyes clouded with a mix of exhaustion and understanding. "All the time," she admitted. "It's like... my thoughts and feelings are constantly colliding. I want to do one thing, but then I question it. I over think everything." She sighed, her shoulders slumping beneath the burden of it all. "It's exhausting."

Aryan nodded, knowing exactly what she meant. "It's like there's a part of you that wants to move forward," he said, "but another part is terrified of making the wrong choice. So you just stay stuck, torn between what you want and what you're afraid of." He paused, his brow furrowed in thought. "It's like being in a storm that never ends."

Meera sighed, her gaze drifting out the window. "You're at war with yourself," she murmured. "That's what it feels like. Constant conflict." Her voice was tinged with frustration, the kind that comes from years of wrestling with indecision and self-doubt. "And it's not just the big things. It's everything. Every little choice, every little feeling—I question it all."

"Why do we do that?" Aryan asked, his voice thoughtful. "Why are we so afraid to trust ourselves? It's like we're always second-guessing, always thinking we'll make the wrong move."

Meera's expression softened, and she turned back to face him. "Because we don't trust ourselves," she said simply. "Or at least, I don't. I don't trust myself to make the right choices. I always feel like… like I'll make a mistake. And then I'll have to live with it."

Aryan's breath hitched at the honesty in her words. He had felt that same fear, time and time again. The fear of taking a step forward, only to realize it was the wrong one. It was paralyzing. And in that paralysis, decisions were delayed, opportunities were missed, and the internal war raged on.

But Aryan had learned something about this war. It wasn't just about decisions; it was about something deeper—a search for the self, an endless quest to understand who he really was beneath the surface. He had fought that war for years, always wondering why the answers eluded him.

"I used to think the battle was about making the right choices," Aryan said quietly, his voice grew thick, heavy with the realization he couldn't deny. "But it's not. It's about finding myself. And that's the hardest battle of all."

Meera blinked, her eyes widening slightly. "Finding yourself?" she echoed, her voice filled with curiosity. "What does that even mean?"

Aryan smiled faintly, his thoughts drifting to the many hours he had spent contemplating that very question. "We hear people talking about 'finding themselves' all the time," he began, "but most of us don't really know what it means, or why it matters. We go through life thinking we know who we are, but the truth is, most of us are just reacting to what's happening around us. We've never really looked inside."

Meera tilted her head slightly, her brow furrowing. "So, what is it then? What does 'finding yourself' mean to you?"

"It's about discovering your true self," Aryan said softly, his voice growing more introspective. "Not the version of you that's shaped by other people's expectations, or by the roles you play in life. But the real you. The person you are when you strip everything else away—the identity that comes from your inner self, not from what's happening outside of you."

Meera's eyes softened, and she looked down, lost in thought. "I don't think I've ever really thought about it that way," she admitted. "I've always just... gone along with whatever was expected of me. I've played the roles I was given, without questioning whether that's who I really am"

Aryan's heart ached at the vulnerability in her words. "That's the trap we all fall into," he said gently. "We spend so much time worrying about what other people want from us, or trying to fit into their expectations, that we lose sight of what we want, who we really are. And when you don't know who you are, everything becomes harder—relationships, decisions, even just living."

Meera sighed deeply, her shoulders sagging under the strain of everything she had kept silent, she felt herself bend. "It's like... I've been living someone else's life," she whispered. "I don't know who I am, Aryan. I've been so busy trying to be what everyone else expects that I've never stopped to ask myself what I want. Who I am."

Aryan reached out, gently taking her hand in his. "That's the first step," he said softly. "Admitting that you don't know. Because once you realize that, you can start searching. You can start asking the questions that matter. Who am I? What do I want? What kind of life do I want to create for myself?"

Meera looked at him, her eyes filled with a mixture of fear and hope. "But what if I don't like the answers?" she asked, her voice trembling slightly. "What if I look inside and I don't like what I find?"

Aryan smiled gently, his expression filled with quiet understanding. "The thing is, once you start this journey, once you start looking inside, you'll realize that there's nothing to be afraid of. Because—your true self—isn't something to fear. It's something to embrace. And the more you embrace it, the more you'll find peace."

Meera's eyes filled with tears, and Aryan could see the struggle written all over her face. She was standing at the edge of something—the edge of a journey that would change everything. But he knew how hard it was to take that first step, to begin the process of self-discovery, especially when you'd spent so long living for other people.

"I've spent my whole life being afraid," Meera whispered, her voice thick with emotion. "Afraid of making the wrong choice, afraid of disappointing people, afraid of failing. But the thing I'm most afraid of... is looking inside and realizing that I've been lost all along."

Aryan's heart ached at the vulnerability in her voice, and he squeezed her hand gently. "You're not lost," he said softly. "You're just on a journey, like the rest of us. And sometimes, it takes losing yourself to find yourself."

Meera nodded, her eyes filling with tears. "I want to find myself," she whispered. "I want to stop living for everyone else. I want to figure out who I really am."

"Then that's the first step," Aryan said gently. "Acknowledging that you're ready for the journey. It's not going to be easy, and it's not something that happens overnight. But every step you take, every time you choose to listen to your own voice instead of someone else's, you're moving closer to the person you're meant to be."

Meera smiled faintly, a glimmer of hope shining through her tears. "I'm scared," she admitted. "But I'm ready."

Aryan nodded, a quiet sense of peace settling over him. "We're all scared," he said softly. "But that's part of the journey. And the more you trust yourself, the easier it gets. You'll learn to listen to your intuition, to trust the sound of your own voice, and to find peace in who you are—without needing anyone else's approval."

The dawn light began to filter through the window, casting a soft, golden glow over the world outside. The train, which had been steadily moving forward, began to slow, the familiar sound of wheels against the tracks growing quieter as they approached a station.

Meera glanced out the window, her eyes filled with the warmth of the early morning light. "Maybe this is our chance," she said quietly. "To stop fighting ourselves. To trust that we can handle whatever comes next."

Aryan smiled, a quiet sense of peace settling over him. "Yeah," he said softly. "Maybe it is."

The train slowed to a stop, and for a moment, they sat in silence, letting the stillness wash over them. It was a new beginning, a chance to leave behind the battles they had been fighting within themselves. The war wasn't over, but maybe, just maybe, they were ready to lay down their weapons and trust themselves to move forward.

As the train came to a halt, the dawn light bathed everything in a soft, golden glow. It was the start of a new day, and with it, a new journey.

A Moment

As the train came to a gentle stop, the steady hum of the wheels against the track faded into the early morning stillness. Aryan stood up, stretching slightly, before turning to Meera with a soft smile. "I'm going to grab something to eat," he said quietly. "Would you like anything?"

Meera shook her head, her voice barely a whisper. "No, I'm fine." She watched him as he stepped off the train, his figure blending into the quiet bustle of the platform. The station was sleepy, with only a few passengers moving around, but there was something in the way Aryan moved—calm, purposeful—that drew her attention.

She watched him as he walked away, a gentle curiosity building in her chest.

Who was Aryan?

The question lingered in her mind as she traced his every step. She had been traveling with him, sharing thoughts and emotions, but there was so much she didn't know about him. So much that remained a mystery.

Meera's thought took wings, she wondered, he would help one, he would help all. That was the kind of person he seemed to be. Someone who gave, without hesitation, without asking for anything in return. He was selfless—always ready to help, to listen, to be there. Meera could see it in the way he spoke, in the way he carried himself. There was a quiet strength in him, but also a deep vulnerability, as if the weight of the world rested on his shoulders and yet, he carried it with grace.

Meera continued to wonder, he feels pain when others get hurt. Meera thought to herself, her gaze lingering on the spot where Aryan had disappeared into the station. "He values every soul around him, at home, in society. But where does he fit into all of this?"

That was the part she couldn't understand. Aryan seemed to give so much of himself—too much, maybe. It was as if he had no value for himself. He seemed to be always ready for anybody, at any time, for anything. But there was also a heaviness in his eyes, a tiredness that spoke of someone who had given so much that there was nothing left for himself. Meera wondered how long he could keep going like that.

"He understands that he's being taken advantage of," Meera thought, her heart swelled with warmth at the realization. "But he doesn't stop. He smiles through it.

He keeps giving, even though people take him for a fool."

There was something heartbreaking about it. Aryan knew—he knew he was overdoing it, knew he was being fooled. And yet, he didn't stop. Meera could see it in his eyes, in the way he held himself. It wasn't that he didn't know. It was that he had made peace with it.

As Meera thought about this, a new understanding began to dawn on her. Maybe it wasn't that Aryan was being foolish. Maybe it was that he understood something the rest of the world didn't. He had come across so many people, all lost in their own way, each of them looking for something they couldn't quite grasp. And Aryan—he had been there to help, to guide, even when they didn't deserve it.

She imagined Aryan meeting someone—someone broken, lost, with all their feelings, emotions, wishes, and dreams pulled out from their soul. She could picture it in her mind—their expressionless eyes, the way they had given up on everything, the way life had robbed them of themselves. They had become so disconnected from their own desires, from the things that once made them feel alive, that they didn't even know what they deserved anymore.

And yet, there Aryan would be, standing before them like a beacon of light, showing them a new path. He would be the torchbearer, guiding them toward something better, something they couldn't see for themselves.

"He wouldn't let them go back to the dark path," Meera thought, her heart swelling with a mixture of awe and sadness. "He holds the light, always pointing forward. He doesn't let them fall back into the life they've accepted, even when they're scared."

That's what he had done for her, she realized with a start. Aryan had been her torchbearer. When she had met him, she had been lost, unsure of who she was, unsure of what she wanted. She had been standing at a crossroad, one road leading back to the life she had known—the life that had made her feel like a stone, numb and disconnected—and the other leading to something unknown, something that scared her just as much as it intrigued her.

Aryan hadn't let her turn back. Every time she had wanted to retreat, to return to the familiar misery she had grown accustomed to, Aryan stood close behind, guiding her forward. He had shown her a new path, a path where she could start to unearth the desires and dreams she had buried so long ago.

And now, as she sat on the train, she saw him for what he truly was. He was her guide, her torchbearer, but he was more than that. He was the reason she had started this journey of self-discovery.

She imagined him standing behind her, holding the light that illuminated the path forward. And yet, in the moments when she had looked back—when she had been too afraid to look at herself—she had seen him. She had seen Aryan, not as the guide, but as the reflection of something beautiful. The way he had helped her see herself, the way he had shown her, her own strength, had made her realize that the beauty she saw wasn't just hers—it was a reflection of the brightness he carried with him.

He was the reason she was starting to trust herself again.

As she continued to gaze out the window, waiting for Aryan to return, Meera couldn't help but wonder: How could someone be so patient, so selfless, so endlessly concerned with others, and yet never ask for anything in return?

"He helped me see myself," she thought, her heart swelling with emotion. "He's still helping me. And all this time, I've been wondering how anyone could be so concerned for so long. But now I see… he doesn't do it for himself. He does it because he can't stand to see people stay lost."

She looked up as Aryan reappeared at the door of the train, holding a small bag of food in one hand. His smile was soft, and as he approached, Meera's heart swelled with gratitude. She wasn't sure she would ever understand him completely, but she knew one thing for certain—Aryan was someone special. He was someone who gave endlessly, even when it hurt, even when people took advantage of him.

"Thank you," Meera whispered, her voice filled with emotion as Aryan sat back down beside her.

Aryan looked at her, his brow furrowing slightly in confusion. "For what?"

Meera smiled softly; her gaze filled with warmth. "For showing me the way."

Aryan's expression softened, and he nodded slowly, though he said nothing. The two of them sat in a comfortable silence, the unspoken truths hanging between them.

As the train prepared to move forward again, the dawn light continued to filter through the window, casting a soft glow over the world outside. It was the start of a new day, and with it, a new journey.

Meera glanced over at Aryan; her heart filled with a quiet sense of peace. She didn't know where this journey would take them, but she knew one thing: they were in it together. And for the first time in a long time, she felt ready to face whatever came next.

The train slowly began to move, and as it left the station behind, Meera and Aryan embarked on their new journey, side by side.

The Fear of Losing

The train's motion seemed different now, slower, more deliberate, it felt as it all the unsaid things were finally catching up with them. Aryan sat in silence, his thoughts heavy, while Meera sat beside him, gazing out the window, lost in her own turmoil. There was a strange kind of tension between them, unspoken but palpable, and it filled the space like a thick fog neither could see through.

Meera's heart was pounding, her mind swirling with a thousand thoughts she couldn't quite organize. Over the past hours, she had felt something shifting between them, something fragile but undeniably real. But now, as they sat side by side, she couldn't shake the feeling that she was on the verge of losing something—someone—she hadn't fully understood yet.

Why was she so afraid? Why did the thought of losing Aryan, someone she had only recently met, fill her with so much fear?

Aryan sensed the shift too, though he couldn't put it into words. He had spent so much time trying to be present, trying to show Meera the way forward, but now, there was an unease gnawing at him—a sense that everything he had tried to build could crumble at any moment. Why did it feel like he was losing her, even though she was sitting right there?

He turned to look at her, his heart glowed at the sight of her face—so serene on the outside, but he knew better. He could see the tension in the way her fingers gripped the armrest, the way her eyes darted across the landscape as if searching for something she couldn't find.

"Meera," Aryan said softly, his voice breaking the stillness. "Are you okay?"

She didn't answer right away, still gazing out the window as if lost in her own thoughts. Finally, after what felt like an eternity, she turned to face him, her eyes filled with an emotion he couldn't quite read.

"I don't know," she whispered, her voice trembling. "I'm scared, Aryan. I'm scared of losing... something. I don't even know what it is, but it feels like if I don't figure it out soon, it'll be gone forever."

Aryan's heart clenched. He understood that fear—the fear of losing someone before you even had the chance to understand what they meant to you. He had felt it before, in other relationships, but this time it felt different. This time, it was deeper.

"Why do we fear losing the people we love?" Aryan mused aloud; his voice soft but steady. "Why does the thought of separation make us so uneasy?"

Meera blinked, caught off guard by the question. "Because when we lose someone," she began hesitantly, "it feels like we lose a part of ourselves. Like we're left incomplete."

Aryan nodded, the depth of her words sinking in. "It's because we're all connected," he said quietly. "Our minds, our hearts, our souls—they're in sync with the people we love. When we feel that connection slipping away, it triggers something deep inside us, something primal. We become afraid. And that fear... it can overwhelm us."

Meera's eyes filled with tears, and she wiped at them quickly, trying to hold herself together. "I don't want to lose you, Aryan," she whispered, her voice breaking. "But I'm so afraid. I'm afraid of letting you in, of trusting this, of trusting you. And at the same time, I'm terrified of losing you before I even understand what this is between us."

Aryan's heart ached at the vulnerability in her words. He could feel the fear radiating off her—the same fear that had lived inside him for so long. The fear of losing someone you don't want to lose.

"I feel it too," Aryan admitted softly. "That fear of disconnection, of separation—it's real. And it's powerful. But it's not the whole story."

Meera frowned, clearly confused. "What do you mean?"

"We only feel that fear," Aryan explained, "because we think we're separate. We think we're different, disconnected from each other. But the truth is, we're all connected. And when we realize that, when we truly understand that connection, the fear starts to fade."

Meera's brow furrowed, her mind racing to understand. "But what if I do lose you?" she asked, her voice filled with quiet desperation. "What if something happens, and you're not there anymore? What do I do then?"

Aryan reached out, gently taking her hand in his. "You don't lose someone just because they're not physically there," he said softly. "When you're connected to someone, that connection doesn't go away. It's eternal. It lives on, even if the physical presence doesn't. The relationship, the influence that person had on your life—it doesn't die. It continues, in your heart, in your memories."

Meera stared at him, her eyes wide with emotion. "But I don't want you to be just a memory," she whispered, her voice shaking. "I don't want to lose you."

Aryan squeezed her hand, his gaze steady. "You won't," he said softly. "Because we're connected. Whether we're together or apart, that connection doesn't go away. It's not just about being physically present. It's about something deeper. Something that goes beyond time, beyond distance."

Meera's tears fell freely now, her breath heavy with the emotions. "But what if I can't handle it?" she whispered. "What if I can't handle the thought of losing you?"

Aryan put his arm around her, holding her tightly as she sobbed against his chest. "You can," he whispered. "You're stronger than you think. And I'm not going anywhere, Meera. But even if something happens, even if we're apart—you're never truly alone. None of us are. The connection—it stays with you. Always."

The train slowed down again, the rhythmic clattering of the wheels fading into the background as the world outside seemed to come to a standstill. Meera clung to Aryan, her tears finally slowing as the truth of his words began to settle over her.

She didn't want to lose him—the thought of it filled her with an almost unbearable sense of fear. But deep down, she knew he was right. The connection they shared wouldn't disappear, even if circumstances changed. It wasn't something that could be broken by time or distance. It was eternal.

"You're right," Meera whispered, her voice still trembling but filled with a quiet strength. "I don't have to be afraid. As long as we're connected, I won't lose you. Even if things change, even if life takes us in different directions—that connection will still be there."

Aryan smiled gently, pulling back slightly to look into her tear-streaked face. "Exactly," he said softly. "We're connected, Meera. And that's something that can never be taken away."

As the dawn light began to fill the train, casting a soft glow over everything, Meera felt a sense of peace settle over her. The fear was still there, lurking beneath the surface, but it no longer consumed her. She wasn't alone.

And even though the future was uncertain, even though she didn't know what lay ahead, she knew one thing for certain: she and Aryan were connected. And that connection would last, no matter what.

As the train slowed down to stop at the station, Meera and Aryan sat together, their hands intertwined, ready to face whatever came next. The fear of losing was still there, but so was the connection, the unbreakable bond that held them together.

The Leap of Faith

The train slowly approached the station, the rhythmic clattering of the wheels gradually fading. Aryan sat quietly, his gaze fixed on the approaching platform, his mind heavy with the weight of everything left unsaid. Meera sat beside him, her heart racing, the familiar knot of fear tightening in her chest.

This was it. His station.

Meera could feel the pull of finality in the air, the sense that once Aryan stepped off that train, everything would change. She glanced at him from the corner of her eye, watching his calm demeanor, the way he seemed so composed. How was he so at peace when she felt like her world was falling apart?

The train came to a halt. The doors hissed open.

Aryan stood up, his movements slow and indeliberate, as if each step toward the door was a calculated decision. He turned to Meera with a soft smile, his eyes reflecting something she couldn't quite name—something that felt like goodbye, but also like hope.

"I guess this is my stop," Aryan said quietly, his voice steady, though there was a slight tremor beneath the surface.

Meera nodded, but her throat felt tight. She tried to speak, to say something—anything—but the words wouldn't come. Instead, she watched as Aryan turned toward the door, his back to her, his figure moving further away with each passing second.

He stepped off the train, his silhouette framed by the sunlight streaming through the open door. The world outside seemed to blur as he took his first steps onto the platform, the distance between them growing.

And suddenly, it hit her like a tidal wave—the fear of losing him. The fear she had been trying to push down, trying to hide behind reason and logic, it exploded inside her, filling every corner of her being with a desperation she had never felt before.

"Aryan!" she choked out, her voice trembling with emotion, but he didn't hear her. He was too far away now, already part of a world she wasn't sure she could follow him into.

Meer's heart pounded violently in her chest, a desperate scream echoing in her mind, urging her legs to move faster. She couldn't lose him. Not this time. Not any time. Her breath came in ragged gasps as she darted towards the door, barely slipping through, as it hissed shut behind her, the metal grazing her back with a finality that sent shivers down her spine.

Inside, her eyes, blurred with tears, frantically scanned the sea of faces. Panic gripped her, the crowd felt like it was swallowing her whole. Her vision darted left, then right, her pulse quickened with every second he was out of sight. She could hardly see through the blur of strangers pushing past, her heart twisting in anguish. Was she too late?

Then, like a beacon through the chaos, her eyes locked onto him, there he was. Aryan standing motionless at the edge of the platform, he looked so far away, so close to disappearing. Her tears flowing freely, as every inch of her body ached to close the distance.

"Aryan!" she cried, feeling the weight of his own experiences settle heavily on his chest.

He stopped, frozen in place by the sound of her voice. Slowly, he turned, his eyes widening in surprise as he saw her standing there, tears streaming down her face, her chest heaving with emotion.

"Meera?" he whispered, his voice soft, but filled with concern.

Before he could say another word, Meera closed the distance between them, her feet carrying her faster than she thought possible. And then, just as he turned fully to face her, she reached out and grabbed his hand, her fingers trembling as they intertwined with his.

"Don't go," Meera gasped, her voice barely above a whisper, but the desperation in it was unmistakable. "Please don't go, Aryan. I can't... I can't let you leave. Not like this."

Aryan's breath caught in his throat, his eyes searching hers, trying to understand the depth of what she was saying. "Meera," he began, his voice gentle, "I didn't think—"

"I'm terrified," Meera interrupted, her voice shaking as more tears fell. "I'm terrified of losing you. I've spent this whole time trying to convince myself that I'd be okay if you left, but... I'm not okay. I won't be okay. I don't want to lose you, Aryan."

Aryan felt a deep unsettling ache, the emotion in her voice slicing through him like a blade. He had always known that there was something between them—something fragile, something unspoken—but hearing her say it out loud, feeling the raw intensity of her fear, it broke something inside him.

"Meera," he whispered, stepping closer, their hands still locked together. "I didn't want to push you. I didn't want to ask for more than you were ready to give. But..." He trailed off, his voice thick with emotion, before he whispered, "I'm terrified too. I'm terrified of leaving you behind. Of what it means if I step off this platform and you're not there with me."

Meera sobbed, her body trembling as she clung to him, her grip on his hand tightening. "Then don't leave," she begged, her voice cracking with desperation. "Stay. Stay with me. I don't know what this is between us, Aryan, but I know I can't lose it. I can't lose you."

Aryan stared at her, his own emotions threatening to spill over as he reached up and gently cupped her face, wiping away her tears with his thumb. "You won't lose me," he whispered, his voice filled with quiet intensity. "I'm right here, Meera. I'm not going anywhere. Not without you."

Meera's breath hitched, her tears slowing as she looked up at him, her heart pounding in her chest. "Promise me," she whispered, her voice trembling. "Promise me you won't leave."

Aryan smiled softly, his forehead resting against hers as he whispered, "I promise."

For a moment, the world around them seemed to disappear. The noise of the station, the distant hum of the train, the people moving around them—it all faded away, leaving only the two of them, standing together on that platform, their hands intertwined, their hearts beating in sync.

Meera closed her eyes, feeling the warmth of Aryan's touch, the steady rhythm of his breathing, and for the first time ever, she felt at peace. The fear that had consumed her—the fear of losing him, of losing everything—began to ease.

"I don't know what happens next," Meera whispered, her voice barely audible.

"Neither do I," Aryan replied softly, his lips brushing against her forehead. "But whatever it is, we'll figure it out. Together."

They stood there for a while, their foreheads pressed together, the world outside the station coming to life around them. The early morning light was soft, casting a gentle glow over the platform. The air was cool, but inside, their hearts were warm, pulsing with a connection that went beyond words, beyond fear.

Slowly, Meera pulled back, her eyes locking with Aryan's. "Where do we go from here?" she asked, her voice still trembling with emotion, but there was a small smile playing at the corners of her lips.

Aryan's fingers tightened around hers, his gaze steady, filled with something unspoken but powerful. "Wherever you want," he said softly. "This was just one journey, Meera. But the real journey starts now."

Together, they turned, stepping away from the train that had brought them to this moment. The platform behind them faded, becoming a distant memory as they walked toward the exit, their hands still intertwined, their hearts beating as one.

The world stretched out before them, filled with endless possibilities, and for the first time, Meera felt no fear. Whatever came next, they would face it together.

As they stepped onto the road ahead, Aryan smiled softly, his voice barely above a whisper. "We're walking toward something new, Meera. A new destination. A new journey."

Meera smiled through her tears, her heart swelling with a quiet certainty. "Yes," she whispered, squeezing his hand. "Together."

The sun climbed higher in the sky, casting a golden light over everything as Aryan and Meera walked side by side, their steps in sync, their future unwritten but filled with hope.

And as they walked away from one journey, they began another—together.

The End

Acknowledgment

I would like to extend my deepest gratitude to Dr. Sunheela K. Ali for her invaluable assistance in proofreading this book.

And to my first readers, my children, (Zohra, Umaays, Zubair & Maisah and to my colleagues, Mouhyi Eddine Lahlali & Imran Abro, whose encouragement and feedback have been instrumental in bringing this book to life. To each of you, your support means the world to me.

Thank you for being a part of this journey.

— Younus Ali

Afterword

*"The characters, Aryan and Meera, were both amazingly depicted. The portrayal of their respective journeys was well justified. It was an emotional experience. The scenic descriptions were spectacular! I have really enjoyed reading the book.
To be honest, there were several points that made me think that I might actually be reading a book from a store (bestselling aisle, of course)
Really glad to be amongst the first to read."*

- *Zohra Hussain*

"It's a beautiful and emotional journey that explores deep emotions. With authentic characters and thoughtful writing, it's a must-read for anyone seeking a reflective and deeply moving story."

- *Imran Abro*

"The Untouched Feeling - speaks to something deeply relatable in all of us. Every man who reads it might see himself in Aryan's struggles and hopes, just as every woman might recognize herself in Meera's quiet strength and resilience. Their journey feels like our own - reflecting the silent battles and vulnerable moments we each experience. Through Aryan and Meera's story, Younus creates a mirror for readers, inviting us to connect with the parts of ourselves that we often keep hidden. This novel is a moving reminder of the power of human connection, especially in the most unexpected places, and of the courage it takes to open up to others and ourselves."

- *Mouhyi Eddine Lahlali*

Recommended for all lovers of literature.

THE NEXT CHAPTER

TEN TINY TWISTY TALES

SUNHEELA KHALID ALI

MA (Eng.), MA (Urdu), B.Com (Comp.), B. Ed.,
Certified Clinical Counselor

"The Next Chapter: Ten Tiny Twisty Tales" is a collection of stories that will enchant you, inspire you, and leave an indelible mark upon your heart.

https://www.amazon.com/NEXT-CHAPTER-TINY-TWISTY-TALES/dp/B0CFZBZD6J

Milton Keynes UK
Ingram Content Group UK Ltd.
UKHW030637191124
451300UK00005B/23